Table of Cor

Introduction...v

Chapter 1: The Role of Influence in Leadership........................1

Types of Influence 4
Understanding Power 6
Power versus Influence 10

Chapter 2: The Power of Influence in Today's Society.........15

Ethical Leadership..17
Ethics of Influence for Today's Ethical Leaders 18
The Transformational Leader.. 20
Contemporary Thought Leaders 25

Chapter 3: How to Build Your Influence 29

Influencing Skills.. 30
3 Keys to Influencing People 31
Major Influencing Approaches.................................... 32
Communicate with influence.. 43

Chapter 4: Influencing Change.......................................49

How to Bring Positive Change in Your Life 52
How to Influence Change in Others.............................. 55
Positively Influence Change at Work 57

Chapter 5: How to Persuade and Influence.......................63

Persuasion Versus Influence 64
Rational Persuasion... 66
Emotional Persuasion 71
The Persuasive Leader 73

Chapter 6: Consultation and Collaborative Approach in Leadership..77

    Consultation: An Influencing Tactic...............................78

    Why Collaboration Matters 80

    Increase Your Collaborative Influence...........................81

    Collaborative Leadership 84

Chapter 7: Inspirational Appeal: Leading With Inspiration, Vision, and Value...89

    Characteristics of an Inspirational Leader 90

    The Art of Inspiring People 95

    The Inspirational Leader 97

Chapter 8: How to Build a Legacy Leadership.....................99

    Principles of Leadership Legacy 100

    Building Leadership Legacy...106

    How I want to influence the world 109

    Keep your Legacy in Check...115

Over to You 119

References 123

Impactful Influence for Modern Leaders

How to Use the Power of Influence to Lead Other People Toward Success

Paul A. Wyatt

Introduction

In retrospect, can you think of an instance at some point in your life when you have wished for an incomprehensible ability to influence others? Individual perspectives may differ, but it is reasonable to say that humans aspire to acquire the necessary qualities to become successful leaders. It is your inner drive and passion that, when channeled in the right way, will make you recognize how vital ambitions are in your life. There may be many opposing views to this notion, but it is never too late to gather your confidence and chase a newly discovered objective or a long-held passion. So, why not envision yourself in a leadership role, and if you already are, why not increase your influence in the most genuine way possible!

The era that we live in is boundless of opportunities, wherein it all lies in your intelligence and effort to achieve what you aim for. No doubt, it does sound a bit far-fetched. But what if I told you that you have all in you to become the successful and influential leader that you have always intended to be? The answer to this question lies in the content that follows gradually. Power is a word that is entrusted with a lot of responsibilities. The prime idea of power lingers on the fact that most leaders are capable of making others look up to their decisions. Power can be at the disposal of the leaders and the heads of any group or department concerned. A person belonging to any sector, be it the government, corporate, political, economic, social, or any other important sector- if you hold a leadership position, you need to understand everything under the sun that is related to the foundation of being an impactful leader who is loved, respected, and most importantly followed widely.

From kings to political leaders, to social leaders to corporate heads, there has been no dearth of leaders throughout the beginning of civilization. There are significant misconceptions that hound the minds of many when it comes to powerful leadership. Some associate being a leader with money, some do with fame, and many with success. However, simply wealth and fame are not what exactly makes a leader who is positively an influential leader. It is a fact that not many can hold the attention of the masses for a long duration, and not everyone has the skill to bring about a strong impact on the people in general.

To have an impact on their teammates, employees, audience, or simply create new friends, everyone, especially a leader, needs to be able to influence people. Many leaders have a significant following, but they somehow fail to retain that influence to motivate and show an efficacious pathway to the people around them. Failure to study the mind's power and the art of persuasion can lead to a slew of problems on the path to realizing one's hopes and goals. The pressure that is built around the idea of understanding this theory can be a daunting task, which may, in the long run, adversely affect the self-confidence of a leader. Furthermore, this is often cited as one of the most common reasons for leadership failure.

The thumb rule for leaders is that they should never disconnect with their people, rather they should never lose even a slight chance to understand the benefit of gaining the trust and faith of people in them. Or else, they could largely put their position at stake. Therefore, a leader must ingest the importance of communicating with others in the most authentic way possible.

Being a leader, no matter how big or small, can be a real backbreaker! You are always under the scrutiny of the higher authorities, the people working for you, the people you intend to guide, the people against your ideologies, the people who are your competition, and many other related sections of the society. A simple mistake can shatter your image. Therefore, you should make a cautious pitch to make an impact in the field that you belong to so that you build a place yourself.

A simple question, the answer to which gives a wholesome picture on the topic that we are debating over is: "What helps in bringing change?". The answer to this, along with various other connotations, is a powerful nudge to 'leadership'! Without powerful leadership, bringing an impact in any field is highly arduous. The chaos and the complexities that may arise from the lack of proper vision and strong guidance from a leader can be burdensome. This is because leaders have to have a strong ability to solve problems without any bias and should be able to handle the minds of the numerous people who follow them or work for them! That requires a great deal of influence!

Power of influence is an intense topic to delve into. It has diverse connotations attached to the theory, some positive and some negative. The point is that people can be leaders in their rights. It is considered a trait that should be one of the dominating characteristics of a leader with some authority. For example, if you are a leader in a corporate business setup and you need to start a new business segment, the first thing you will require is to get your team heads and employees on board with your idea. The resources you may require, the budget allocations, permits, employees' mindset, etc., every aspect requires influence because it is nearly impossible to sell your ideas without having a grip on your target audience's mind! More so, there can be numerous challenges that one may face as a leader, and the biggest of them all is to deal with a diverse kind of people regularly. It can get extremely tricky and can be a matter of sensitivity. To achieve the goal of influencing more and more people does require an array of strategies.

Some of the renowned leaders and influential figures that we have seen throughout history are, to name a few, Martin Luther King, Jr., Nelson Mandela, Abraham Lincoln, Mahatma Gandhi, Winston Churchill, Marie Curie, Henry Ford, and the like. These personalities could not be bound by demarcations and borders. They achieved gigantic success to shape the story of the world in many different impactful ways. One of the common reasons why they became quite famous was that they won the hearts of the masses, and by doing so, they raised the bar pretty high for several other figures to reach.

No border, religion, color, or creed can come in the way of the credibility of a leader. So, how does one hone one's capabilities to become a gold-rated leader? Leadership can be full of momentum and can be exasperating at times. There is no scope of losing control or patience when dealing with people for whom you are a leader. Communication and marketing of one's strategy requires a lot of manipulation, which may sound negative, but has many aspects attached to it. Trustworthiness has to go hand in hand with the authoritative role that a leader possesses. To lead a bunch of people, you have to be open to the idea that you have to be able to market your ideas to a large section of people, and yes, selling is a difficult task! Take a moment and think about an instance like the voting system in democratic countries. How does a single person end up becoming the most powerful person in the entire country by becoming the head of the governmental order? How is it possible for the leaders to convince the majority of the people in the country to simply go and cast a vote in their favor? Every answer will hint toward the role of influence!

Therefore, if you are seeking to improve your leadership skills and grow as a professional in any sector, you have to understand the concept of power and the deep-rooted aspect of influence. It is not worth drowning in the pool of your self-doubts. Rather, it is time to learn new skills to grow and unlearn anything that has been coming on your way to becoming a successful and impactful leader. Every second counts, and the effort that you make by following the guidance laid meticulously in this book will help you achieve your dream of becoming a stronger version of yourself and most significantly becoming a leader who is powerful and influential to the core!

1

The Role of Influence in Leadership

How many times have you been compelled to attend long and arduous meetings and seminars hosted by your workplace's senior management? How many times have you worried about sitting through a dull lecture? How many times have you believed that receiving motivational quotes via email is preferable to meeting with your leaders in person? How many times have you failed to get inspired by your leaders, yet you just nod your head in approval out of fear of some sort? How many times have you imagined that if you had more power to influence others, you could make a bigger difference? The answer to these questions varies from person to person, and it also hinges on what and how a leader should be in order to exert that degree of control and influence on the audience. However, the point is that you meet several people in your life, but not many can have the impression of an influential leader. Leadership does not always have to be associated with high-ranking government posts, corporate behemoths, or politics. An individual can be a leader in his or her own right, with the ability to influence a large number of people and pave the way for change.

Peter F. Drucker, in his work "Your Leadership is Unique", says, "The only definition of a leader is someone who has followers. Some people are thinkers. Some are prophets. Both roles are important and badly needed. But without followers, there can be no leaders." This insightful statement throws some light on the meaning and significance of being a leader. It is not about the hierarchical position or magnificent tags that one possesses. It is about having the aura and skill of a leader who has the potential to be influential and powerful at the same time.

Influence is a concept that is triggered by the power of an individual to bring a change in another's behavior. According to Robert B. Cialdini in his book "Influence, The Psychology of Persuasion", there are six vital techniques mentioned that can be applied in influencing people to agree or rather, say yes. Persuasion is a skill that can be segregated with the principles of reciprocity, social proof, liking, consistency, scarcity, and commitment.

It is often a daunting task to get the required compliance from business associates, partners, colleagues, family, and friends. There is an interesting theory that says that the existence of power is a result of the influence of a dependent relationship.

To pursue the skill of creating an influential aura, you will need the grit and determination to do something that can make a great impact on the minds of people in a constructive way. It is also true that most of the time, we do not become aware of how we have been influencing people around us. Influence can be contagious. For example, when we were children, most of our elders would tell us to not mingle with some and to mingle with some of our friends. Furthermore, they would stress the fact that we would get influenced in a certain way which they, of course, did not approve of. We have been coming across the concept of the power of influence in our day-to-day lives for a very long time.

Leadership cannot be confined to one position or stature. It can be defined with a varied outlook. For example, in a business setup, a leader can be the head of the company who is also the founder and the driving force behind the vision or an appointed CEO. In a political setup, the head of the organization is the leader. In simple words, anyone who can lead a large group of people can be called a leader.

Defending a cause worthy of effort, mobilizing a group towards success, and also setting an example of inspiration are some of the expected traits of a leader. As Bill Gates said, "We look ahead into the next century, leaders will be those who empower others." Thus, it can be said that the term leadership can be explained in many different ways by different people. However, the crux remains the same. Leaders cannot be successful until they learn the art of influencing others.

Influence goes hand in hand with persuasion and reciprocation. Isn't it intriguing enough to understand how and what factors lead a person to affirm another's ideas or suggestions without any speck of hesitation? To achieve this level of compliance can often seem like an impossible task. What if I told you that it is how you use the power of influence that can make your work done, as per your way? Before plugging into the pool of guidance, let's take a look at the different types of influences and how effective they can be to persuade others.

Types of Influence

Not every person thinks in the same manner as the other. No matter how hard one tries, it can take quite a bit of effort to get your influence as a leader on point.

Rational Influence

Be it in business or any other field, logic is what counts. An idea cannot just run on the fuel of theories. It has to be pragmatic and should prove its way towards fulfilling its goals. As a leader, a rational approach can help in presenting your points and arguments with transparency that are supported by facts and not just thoughts. Communicating with your followers by emphasizing the course of actions that can reap positive benefits should be done with confidence and clarity. Influencing the minds of your seniors, peers, and followers has to be made with proper persuasion techniques. The tact needed for this act will require the correct usage of words upheld by proper plans on the table.

Inspirational Influence

It is a mandate that leaders should be inspiring and worthy of being the voice of their followers. If the followers fail to resonate with your ideas, then the uphill climb to becoming a successful leader can be extremely tedious. You, as a leader, are expected to have an effect on your followers, which can compel them to bring about transformational changes. This effect is more about creating an appeal, or rather, influencing others in an inspirational way. The idea is to create a mark on the emotions of people so that they can feel related to a situation. If the leaders can communicate and make the rest understand their vision for the future in a motivating manner, then they can garner immense support and enthusiasm from their followers. One of the most pertinent ways in which they can bring a spark of overwhelming support for their ideas as a leader is by setting themselves as a role model. Their behavior, mannerisms, and ethics will always be under the intense scrutiny of everyone around them. If the leaders set an example by doing the right thing, others following will also be inspired enough to back them up to achieve the collective goal in the long run.

Consulting Influence

Consultation and healthy discussion can bring many benefits towards the achievement of a collective goal. Seeking advice and gathering professional suggestions can also help people understand the challenges involved in a workspace or a political arena. Encouraging the active participation of followers in matters of importance can give them a boost of motivation, thus creating more zeal to perform better. However, when employing consultation as a means of persuasion, the leaders must be on their toes to avoid appearing to be manipulative. It is an influence tactic that has been deployed for many years by leaders of top positions.

Collaborative Influence

The technique of influence through collaboration is a very effective way of making others think and work in a particular way, without making it very evident. In this method, you do not request any form of support; rather, you are in a position to guide and provide assistance. It is a psychological trick that is used most often in the downward or lateral structure of the organizational set-up. Most leaders follow this technique. They provide their subordinates with the resources that they think are appropriate and suggest that they take action as per their guidance. A mutually respectful ambiance is created with the exchange of ideas, and the leader successfully manages to influence the minds of the other people who work for them.

Therefore, it can be seen that persuasion plays a decisive role in the smooth function of a leader's agenda towards the vision and mission goals. Leaders have to have influential powers, and failing to do so, they cannot become as great as some of the well-known leaders in the world.

Understanding Power

Power is a strong word having numerous connotations, and how it has the potential to bring changes in the social and other subordinate aspects has to be examined thoroughly. Power in society is mostly related to the potential of a figure who can bring a significant reform. Such leaders mostly rely on the resources that are available to them, and such resources are mostly related to the six bases of power: reward, legitimate, informational, coercion, expertise, and referent. How social change is accomplished, the length of the change effect, and how power is established are the defining elements of these six bases of power. However, two of the most fundamental bases of power are taken into account as follows:

Formal Power

The position a person holds can be directly proportional to the amount of power entrusted to them. It is a fact that several sources lead to the establishment of formal power. Some of these sources are:

- Legitimate Power: In an organizational setup, power is vested on the higher level of the hierarchical order. This is done to help and monitor the predominant resources to accomplish the vision and goals. Thus, legitimate power is bestowed on topmost officials with complete authority to oversee the working of the business and the employees at large. For example, the Managing Director or the CEO of a company are mostly given the authority to hire and fire employees as per the respective company's norms. They are most often entitled to travel in business class and stay in luxurious hotels. The benefits that a person reaps from the position with full legality can also fall under this category of power.

- Coercive Power: This type of power is also related to legitimate power. The term coercive itself denotes some form of intimidation and threat used in the process of achieving some goal. For example, in an organizational workspace, the topmost authority or the high- managerial posts are given ample power to demote and issue warnings against employees subordinate to them. This form of power has a more negative connotation attached to it, and it is mostly to do with levying punishment or withstanding punishments. It is highly recommended that such power should be used with utmost cautiousness. Negative punishments like issuing suspension, termination orders, and also negatively assigning wrong and unpleasant assignments can all bring repercussions in the long run.

- Reward Power- A type of power that can bestow positivity and motivation among people and followers. This power gives the leaders and the higher authorities the supreme authority to reward their subordinates. Rewards are often given in the form of pay raises, higher increments, promotions, recognitions, praise, and also by assigning important assignments to worthy individuals. Though this type of power has its limitations, an overflow of praise and awards can sometimes have an impact on the goal and make people delusional. However, with the right judgment and correct rewards at their disposal, leaders can pave the way to motivate their followers and subordinates to a great extent. Appreciation of work and positive feedback can encourage a person more than formal rewards. Therefore, by following a concept of upliftment of team spirit and perseverance, a leader can take the team to a high-performing standard in no time.

Hence, it can be said that power comes with a weight of authority and responsibilities. With legitimate powers in hand, leaders can reach a level that can be fruitful for their career as well as their repute.

Informal Power

Informal power is the potency that a person can achieve through influence with the help of personality skills, knowledge, and tact.

- Expert power: It is often noticed in a workspace that an individual or a group of individuals are called experts, and much consultation is taken from them by the authorities and the employees in general. There is a widespread perception that they have a skill set that makes them more knowledgeable about a certain segment of work or anything related to it. This power that is vested in such people has the foundation of superior expertise that they possess. More so, there is a huge dependency on such individuals, which makes them more powerful than the rest of the lot.

- Charismatic Power: The exuberance of power from a person's personality can be very influential in laying a strong foundation for building communication to gain more followers. If leaders possess charismatic charm as well as oratory skills, they are bound to lead a large group of eager followers, which may be beneficial to the overall goal and vision of the organization, and especially the leaders. At the end of the day, it is the personality of the leader that is noticed at first by the rest of the people.

- Referent Power: This form of informal power requires fame and attention. Any person associated with movies, television, sports, music, and so on will have a large audience. Reach through such mediums is comparatively much higher than via any other medium. Their influence cannot be underestimated, and such people with a high referent power will have a considerable amount of potential to access resources and can possess a high impact on the people they intend to influence.

Therefore, it is understood that the concept of power requires various kinds of tactics which can translate power bases into the aimed goals of the leader and other related higher authorities involved in the complex game of power.

Power versus Influence

A wide range of versions of the definition of leadership and power can be found, and one common factor that is often found in all the explanations is the role of influence. Leadership and power are almost synonymous with a very delicate line of demarcation, which even tends to blend with ease in many instances. Power and Influence are two vital aspects of leadership, but with a transparent look into the intricacies of both, it can be said that they have different ways of working. Furthermore, it has to be noted that to create a legacy of leadership, both are of equal importance.

In simple words, with power, you can make a huge, drastic impact on your followers or subordinates. For example, you can ask your followers for opinions, and they would immediately respond with a nod, implying yes, then it can be because of one reason that they respect your position or fear of getting laid off in the long run as a repercussion of their honest opinions. On the contrary, in the case of influence, no such direct impact can be made on people. One can only influence by creating awareness, inspiration, and by motivating the minds of the followers to induce them to agree to something.

Similarly, here are a few differences that draw the thin line between power and influence:

- Influencer leaders have a higher degree of success than power leaders: Influence is transmissible and can spread rapidly like wildfire. Leaders with influential mannerisms are more likable by their followers, as they appear to be relatable and much more approachable than leaders who are just loaded with power. Inspiration is the key to igniting the minds of your followers. Every person has the idea of their leader being someone who they can look up to and strive to become like. Motivation is the key idea behind the implementation of this strategy. It is up to the leaders to strike a deal with followers subtly without making it look like any form of coercion or manipulation, which might look like it in the case of powerful leaders who function only with power.

- The common point of interest that influential leaders may work on with their followers can make them understand their perspective on a closer level. This could have a huge impact on their overall achievement. They will be able to understand the crux of the situation or rather, of any problem, then accordingly act with a positive impact, and most importantly, with the support of their followers. However, on the other hand, leaders who are only power-driven can fail at times to increase the motivation of their followers. They will have a stern work ethic which will make them seek to control, and this might often lead to an abuse of influence. Most power-driven leaders are seen to work through the manipulation of control and ways of subduing processes. This can create an ambiance of fear among subordinates, which can severely impact their overall productivity.

- Influence can be stronger compared to power in several aspects. It is all about the mind and its control of emotions and the entire psychological aspect of humans. Influence-driven leaders are more about serving as a mentor by reaching a large group of people to encourage and bring about a positive impact. They are always on the run to make people get inspired by their vision and goals. Influence leaders are open-minded people who take all kinds of feedback regarding their role, work, position, or any other situation that may be of concern.

- Influence leaders are visionaries and believe in working by drawing out the greatness in all those they deal with. They create an atmosphere that can make their followers safe and respected. On the other hand, power leaders can hardly achieve the willing support of the followers of influence leaders by just dominating and giving commands.

It is a fact that influence can be more beneficial for the organization or the leader's present or future goals, but it cannot also be denied that power and influence, if used together, can bring a drastic change in the minds and behavior of the people who follow. The force that power uses is strenuous when it comes to the smooth and gliding manner in which subtle influential persuasion can do. Influence can be a savior when making decisions of importance and risk. Thus, it can also be assumed that a leader should, or rather must master the qualities of a leader who is powerful and, at the same time, very influential.

As a leader, you can strengthen your bond with your organization and your subordinates by working tactfully. In an enterprise, or any organizational setup for that matter, a leader will require a lot of power at some point in time. More so, you may even be required to influence your audience and make an impact on their minds. Therefore, it will be a wise decision to start building influence, which will help you in many ways.

According to a survey by Glint on the State of Employee Engagement 2020, it is believed that around 44% of human resource professionals claim that many employees give long extra hours at work, not because they are overloaded with work, but because they feel the zeal to do more work. They put in discretionary effort, all because of the influence and motivation that they receive at work. Power, on the contrary, rarely has the potential to make employees give more than required on their plates.

Most of us must have experienced engagement activities in our workplaces. There are times when some of the activities can be extremely fun, and other times, they can be an overwhelming experience. If we think about the reasons that make us repel a certain type of engagement, we might notice that most activities that we are compelled to participate in by our higher authorities may feel exasperating. It may be so that the compulsion that comes along can cause bouts of anxiety and unwillingness in people. But, the activities that we participate in with our own will might be fulfilling and much more rewarding. Anything that is forced upon us, we will naturally try to repel it, but if we are truly motivated to work on something, then that can hardly fail. Inspiration and influence are considered to stay for a very long period and can have a lasting impact on the minds of the people.

Leaders of today should always realize the importance of working by using power and influence in an amalgamated form. They should learn from the mistakes some of the leaders have made by forcefully manipulating the actions of the followers. Leaders should always be aware that only by influencing and inspiring the masses will they be able to maintain power for an extended period of time.

2

The Power of Influence in Today's Society

The ambiance that we are surrounded by plays a crucial role in defining our vibe. The influence of the people around us, be it friends, family, or colleagues, can be so subtle but, at the same time, very strong that we hardly realize that we are being influenced in this manner. Just take a look around you since the time you were a child. Haven't you been influenced by the environment that you were brought up in and the friends that you grew up with? The answer has a high probability of being affirmative. Study carefully, and you will see that you are friends with people who have similar goals and likings. It may be the literature that you prefer or the movies that you watch. Influence can have layers and can play an equally complex role in shaping one's life!

The prime question lies in the fact that the influences that you are dealing with are ethical or unethical. More so, in leadership roles, ethics and influence are major and very significant factors. Cass R. Sunstein, in his book "The Ethics of Influence", mentions that, from an ethical perspective, there is a vast dissimilarity between coercion and influence. Force can be used in many unethical ways. The word 'force' itself is a tad bit unethical. For example, when managers force employees to work for three days at a stretch, they often do so by threatening to fire them. In such cases, to save their job, the employees will no doubt work as asked. This is done in terms of forced influence, but in terms of mere influence, the scenario is never so harsh. As Cass R. Sustain points out, you can always refuse a beggar on the street to give any money. That is your decision to be made, and all that a beggar can do is to try to influence you to a certain extent. Several cases like these can bring about a difference in these two concepts. However, if further evaluated, it can be seen that ethics does play a major role in the leadership quality of a person in a position to lead others.

Ethical Leadership

Ethical leadership is about the code of conduct that is acceptable on professional and moral grounds. It is pertinent to study both the aspects, negative and positive traits of involving ethical up hearing in terms of developing a foundation of the leadership quality that a leader of today would vest in. Ethical leadership and its influence are based on the following significant traits:

Be the example:

Leaders, disregarding the era that they belong to, have to have the ability to inspire the people by setting up an example of themselves. They should not just be fluent in oratory skills, but should be able to practice what they preach. Most people look up to their leaders with an eye of hope and belief, but if the leaders fail to stand up for and against their people, then that will be a big loss in the long run. Traits like loyalty, confidence, honesty, loyalty, etc., all add up to the overall positive aura of the leader. It is a fact that people are more likely to be attracted to leaders with whom they can resonate and can trust for the betterment of their future. Integrity and ethical behavior can not only help leaders survive and win many professional battles, but can help in their personal lives as well.

Communicate

Communication is the foundation of any kind of relationship. Numerous conflicts in the world have been caused by the lack of proper communication or miscommunication. It is very important for a leader with a vision to bring transformational changes, to be precise and clear while communicating with the followers. Humans differ in nature and behavioral patterns. Some people prefer communicating through calls, emails, letters, and, nowadays, more through texts and phone messages. It does not matter what medium people choose to communicate. It is how and why they feel the need to communicate that adds to the gist of the case. With open conversations, leaders will be able to get a transparent view of their followers. They will be more understanding of their issues and feedback. Building relationships based on communication can take eons. However, the idea remains that if leaders can communicate to their followers with honesty, fairness, compassion, and most importantly, respectful communication, the idea of a perfect world of a good relationship between the leader and the followers is born.

Emphasize the Importance of Ethics

An ethical leader has to focus on the crucial factor of using ethical standards in the day-to-day operations of the business and other related matters. A proper code of ethics is a must to survive with full rights in a business or a workplace setup. A fair and professional ambiance can be achieved only through stressing the role of ethics in framing the strong foundation of a leader's character, as well as the overall business setup.

Ethics of Influence for Today's Ethical Leaders

Ethics of influence in today's leaders can never be overruled and has to be abided by with respect and maturity. How and to what extent ethical leadership can bring an impact can be understood by delving deeper into the following points:

- Leaders with a mindset guided by a code of ethics help society and their followers in countless ways. In a formal governmental or corporate setup, a leader has to keep in the back of mind the overall wellbeing of the people who work for him, and most importantly, trust and follow him.

- They have to be aware of the situation and the issues related to the functioning of the core individuals, their team, and the entire organization that they represent. By creating a positive environment and thus building a nurturing relationship with the people who work for them, leaders can garner more support for themselves in exchange as well.

- Creating an environment that encourages positivity and motivation is a vital responsibility of an ethical leader. People in a workspace tend to yield high productivity if the team bonding and ethics are in the right place.

- Respect is one of the most important essential aspects of maintaining relationships, be it in the professional sphere or the personal sphere. No two people can communicate well if there is no respect between the two. A leader has to make sure that a productive working environment is created by showing examples of the ways an ethical organization should work towards a combined goal.

According to the Harvard Business Review, there is a new model for ethical leadership that has the potential to bring more value to societal functions as a whole. This new model talks about how an ethical leader should refrain from just creating a list of 'don'ts', rather priority should be made to create value for society. Max H. Bazerman argues in this utilitarian theory that philosophical ideas should be amalgamated with the pragmatism of business ethics, and by doing so, numerous managerial tasks can be performed pragmatically and ethically. However, to make this idea a success, the leaders involved should bring in cognitive measures to check if there are any form of barriers that may be preventing the people in managerial or higher authorities from making ethical decisions.

As per a publication of Villanova University, there is a 4-V model that aligns with the idea of ethical leadership. This model is a blend of Values, Vision, Voice, and Virtue, the four main characteristics that make a strong leader but most importantly, ethical. Therefore, by using intuitive and deliberative theories and thought processes, leaders who have an ethical approach can work in a much more responsible manner in the long run.

The Transformational Leader

Leadership cannot be limited to one type of leader. Numerous types of leaders can be recognized in the world that we all live in. Some leaders are all about motivation and drive, whereas some work by taking risks and challenges to a higher level. Whatever their style may be, one characteristic that has to be marked common among all is the ability to inspire and bring a remarkable transformation in any sphere that is required the most.

This digital era has brought about several new aspects in the functioning of most organizations. Transformational leadership is one of the most discussed forms of leading that has come to the forefront in recent years. Transformational leaders are those people who lead the order in hopes and aspirations to bring meaningful change. Motivation is the key to engaging the workforce of any setup, and that is what a transformational leader aims to do. Transformational leadership is also considered a significant aspect of the Full Range Leadership Model.

Theorist on leadership and presidential scholar James McGregor defined the essence of transformational leadership in the year 1978. He explained further how leaders and their followers in certain situations support each other and work towards the achievement of mutually aimed goals and success. Many theories say that the designation of a leader is granted by the 'led'. Among the many theories based on transformational leadership, Bernard M. Bass' theory is the most accepted throughout. In his theory, he says that successful transformational leaders should be rated, or rather, their ability should be measured in terms of the impact that they have on their followers. The selfless acts of the leaders, in ways of persevering together with the followers, can boost a feeling of mutual trust, respect, and loyalty between the leader and the followers. Transformational leaders have to be captivating enough to keep their team together in the long run.

In his work called "Lincoln the Transformational Leader", Gordon Leidner talks about American history regarding the leadership qualities of Abraham Lincoln, the 16th President of America. Ample work based on Lincoln can indeed be found around the world, but not many have been written based on a modern leadership theory that would make an effort to analyze the leadership skills of Lincoln.

To evaluate the transformational leadership of Lincoln, his capabilities were studied and measured in three different ways by:

- Understanding the level of trust, respect, and loyalty acquired by Lincoln from his followers.

- Understanding how he inspired his followers and motivated them to make difficult sacrifices, even in the hardest of times.

- Understanding how ethically he influences his followers to maintain a sense of high morality.

The Army of the Potomac documented the opinions of their soldiers about Lincoln in the form of letters and writings, which are available even to this day. Most of these letters by the soldiers were addressed to their close ones, like family and friends. If taken a closer look, it can be felt that their opinions presented about Lincoln were real and heartfelt. Lincoln was a leader whom people looked up to, and thus, he had an enormous bunch of support behind him to take him towards the achievement of their shared objectives and goals.

Author William C. Davis believes that Lincoln took a big initiative to stay in close contact with the soldiers. Since he had already served as a volunteer at the Blackhawk War, he was familiar with the ways of the army, as well as their hierarchical approaches. He had seen the struggles of these army men closely because of which he had an empathetic approach on issues related to the same. The point is that in order to affect a significant change and a wave of positive influence in the minds of his followers, a leader must attend to the smallest details of the problems they face.

William Seward, Secretary of State, made a quote about Lincoln which says, "There was never a man so accessible to [both] proper and improper persons." This sums up the whole point! The involvement of Lincoln in anything related to the concerns of the distressed soldiers is just an example to show how a transformational leader should act. The common touch and the approachable attitude of the president then flocked more and more people towards his aura.

One question that does arise at this juncture is: What are the vital habits that leaders have to inculcate within them to become successful transformational leaders? Here are a few traits that are essential for leaders to bring noteworthy changes:

Self-Awareness

Reflecting on one's strengths and weaknesses can help a person achieve a deep sense of self-awareness. The prime quality of transformational leaders is to focus on the overall growth of the organization or the team they work with, along with consistent self-improvement. Habits that appear small, like setting daily goals, can look unimportant, but they are exactly the practices that can help leaders plan and focus on their primary objectives. The eagerness to learn and the passion to get the best outcome from the efforts made are some of the dominant traits that a leader must possess to bring about positive reform.

Management skills

Management skills are a prerequisite for the role of a leader, be it in any field. They should be firm in making decisions but should also be able to understand the minds of their subordinates and peers while doing so. They should be self-sufficient and be able to work with a minimum of external influence. To bring about a transformation, a leader has to be empathetic and, at the same time, skillful enough to have a strong grip on the team and followers.

Visionary

Every leader must be a visionary with targeted goals and objectives. Transformational leaders have to be able to motivate the followers by influencing them with their ideas and vision for the organization. They should spread enthusiasm and create an ambiance of support and inspiration among the followers. No goal can be achieved without a set of proper plans or a right vision. Transformational leaders have to be aware of the serious-ness of their goals and must strive to work towards them with full dedication.

Innovative

Innovation is the key to bringing a real transformation. Without thinking out of the box, no one can discover a new path towards success. Transformational leaders can bring a change only if they are bursting with ideas about bringing attainable growth. They should think with hindsight and should never fear taking a risk to try out well-researched strategies.

Therefore, it can be seen how transformational leaders are capable of bringing a change in regular business dy-namics and can mark their way towards success employ-ing continuous learning and collaborating with their followers.

Transformational leaders are visionaries who look to-wards building a successful future. They utilize numerous techniques and strategies to take their company in a direction that will yield fruitful outcomes. They also deploy ideas that make them stay ahead in the race of competition. They are known for their adaptability skills which keep them moving even in the most difficult hours.

Contemporary Thought Leaders

The era of today is marked by the influential role of the so-called Millennials and, most recently, the Generation Z category of people. Technological advancements have broadened their horizons to the point where it is difficult to find someone these days who does not have a mobile phone in their hand! With visible changes in the way of living and the wide footprint of people on the internet, it can be assumed that it is the booming times of the digital and internet era.

It is needless to say that most of us are aware of all the social platforms available and are, to a certain extent, ardent followers and users too. In recent times, there has been an influx of 'influencers' in the sphere of social media and other internet mediums. The biggest brands and companies in the world have also laid down their foundation to establish smooth relationships with some of the prominent influencers the digital market has seen. Adaptability is a virtue, and it is during such a change in the structure and functioning of people all around the world that it is needed even more.

It has to be noted that, when talking about generations, Gen-Z is very different in comparison to Millennials in terms of their attitude and opinions. No matter what, these are the sections of the people that are helping to bring a modern thought leadership pattern to bear. There are several reasons why influencers are considered more effective than a conventional type of leading a group of followers. They are all leaders in their way. They know how to deal with the masses to gain more attention. The various trending social media applications and sites like Twitter, Instagram, Facebook, YouTube, and even Pinterest, etc., have no doubt seen a spike in the rise of people who are termed as influencers.

The power of influence is based on an energy that is given fuel by people's reactions and comments. This logic is used in a very cognitive manner to set up a base of influencers in such mediums on the internet. Over the last few years, the internet has witnessed a revolutionary change. Most people no longer prefer to read the newspapers, people prefer to purchase products online rather than go to a shop, people would rather follow a relatable person for fashion or makeup advice than watch an advertisement of a Hollywood star showing unachievable beauty standards. The profound juncture that makes the minds of the followers meet the ideas of the influencers is the feeling of relatability.

Modern-day influencers are often referred to as social media celebrities or stars because their popularity can be tremendously huge! Digital marketing is one of the areas where such influencers play a mind-shattering role which seems surreal but is true. Every few seconds, a person has access to the internet, where they will see some form of marketing, subtle or direct, taking place. Influencers of today have created a niche of their own in their respective fields and have similar kinds of followers. It is believed that they also have the potential to make or break your product campaign in a matter of one post that they share. According to Forbes, micro-influencers are the future of the marketing industry. These influencers normally have

1,000 to 100,000 followers, and they all primarily use common social media platforms.

In the case of any form of leadership, influence and accessibility have a profound role. The level at which most modern-day influencers are accessible to the wide world is what makes them successful and, at times, susceptible to a few disadvantages as well. While they have the capability to influence a majority of the people with their niche category of content, at the same time, miscreants lurk around on the internet too, who can create more havoc than any good in the long run. With too much endorsement pressure from brands, some influencers tend to lose their authenticity in the long run. Numerous fashion and cosmetic influencers tend to work as per a brand's requirements, which, if not done in a subtle manner, may cause a loss of many of their followers due to the generation of a feeling of manipulation.

At the end of the day, it does not matter how big a star you are or how famous a celebrity you are. Being a leader is a role that can bring ample challenges, but with the right choices and correct influences, one can become a genuine leader who can bring massive positive reforms in the organization, community, and societal space.

3

How to Build Your Influence

Let's just take a pause and think of a particular trait of a leader that can be considered the most essential. It is quite evident that everyone will end up with different answers, but it can also not be denied that influence is one major factor that can take a leader to an altogether bigger standard. Influence can have different connotations. Many would generally assume it to be a factor that requires a lot of scheming and negative manipulation. Though that cannot be denied completely, it is also a fact that there are a few key strategies that, when combined, can make you master the skill of influencing others as a strong leader.

It is quite a difficult task to subject leadership to one type of role or designation. The CEO of a corporate firm, the principal of a high school, team leader, department manager, heads of government bodies, and the like can all be termed as leaders. However, it is their ability to garner influence from their clients, vendors, subordinates, and peers that gives them the lead to earning professional repute and respect.

Influencing Skills

Influencing skills are the skills that make you thrive in a world that is high in competition. It is the skill that makes you persuade and make others behave as per your ideas and instructions. It is not necessarily that this skill is used aggressively to force down authority on subordinates, but more of how, by using a subtle approach, you can motivate and mark a spot in the minds of others. To elaborate it further, let us understand a few effective strategies that can be used in curbing the path for a leader to become all the more influential in the long run.

3 Keys to Influencing People

According to an article by the Center for Creative Leadership, the key tactics considered to be the most beneficial for influence can be segregated into three major categories using the medium of the head, heart, or hands. Let us further plunge into the details:

Logical Appeal (Head)

This falls into the category of the first key tactic for influence. The head signifies the intellectual and rational factors of a human persona. It is the mind that helps one make a logical decision or put together an effective argument based on benefits that may be personal or professional. Leaders have to have the ability to tap into the thoughts of their subordinates and followers. It can be a rather daunting task to manipulate the minds of the people without placing a logical explanation for any idea, method, or vision that needs to be worked on as a collective goal. Hence, leaders will not be looked upon if they just promise magnanimous goals, but rather will be respected when they place a transparent approach with valid points in front of their followers. Persuasion is done the best when it is backed up with rational conclusions.

Emotional Appeal (Heart)

Most humans are, by nature, a tad bit emotional, and more often, the heart takes over the mind while making any serious decisions. An emotional appeal has a stronger effect than can be imagined. Therefore, leaders have to be able to communicate with their followers, striking at the correct emotional spot. The skill of projecting an idea or a goal strategy by communicating with the people involved and making it relatable and valuable is what a leader should always look forward to. Making a connection with the people, heart to heart, can make a leader feel more humane and more in touch with the reality of the followers. This sense of belonging can be an excellent factor which can help leaders understand the real problems and thoughts of their subordinates. No doubt, a positive vibe of good service can always gather more and, most importantly, genuine followers.

Cooperative Appeal (Hands)

A successful leader will always vouch for the benefits of collaboration. Leaders cannot ever function alone without support from their subordinates and followers. The consultation and cooperation between the leader and their alliances are what bring a massive sense of credibility. A leader should never question the intellect of the followers. They should never be taken for granted. Mutual respect and a feeling of camaraderie can always give a push of support for the leader. By extending a helping hand towards others, leaders can effectively create a positive vibe, which can bring them more success as influential leaders.

Major Influencing Approaches

There are more to the above-mentioned three categories of tactics. Without proper strategies, it is not feasible for any plan to fall into place. The question that is bound to hit an aspiring leader in this case is as to how these tact theories can be used in the first place. To make the answer simple and much more understandable, here is a list of seven major approaches that can be used by leaders, or those aiming to become one, to garner power for influence and achieve the desired goal:

Strategic Influence

Any effort made without valid and functional strategies can always have a risk of developing or hidden loopholes. Strategic influence is a type of technique that can be used by a leader to build connections, rapport, credibility, skills, and even the required infrastructures with an intention to win future goals. This leadership style can be applied in various other arenas apart from just business and career. Personal and social goals can also be made easier to achieve by applying this approach. The influence that can be generated with the help of such strategies can make it possible for leaders to give a new direction to the process and trend of the business industry if need be.

Strategic influence is not just a fad theory that has recently come to play. It is a technique that has been used for many years. A leader has to note that in business or any other organizational setup, the skill to lay down plans, implement those plans, and further influence the minds of the people to execute those plans requires a great deal of strategy and perseverance. Every leader has to be agile enough to understand the working and market situation of the business that they are involved in. Building influence strategically is not at all an easy job. A leader has to maintain relationships that are built on a foundation of trust and loyalty. An understanding of the diverse networks that are involved in building public relations with the targeted followers and audiences is a must for a leader to become a leader who can influence positively. Strategic influence has many benefits. It can be used for the following purposes as well:

- Strategic influence can be beneficial in laying the foundation of strong professional relationships.

- It can help create a positive impact on the image and reputation of the leaders.

- Extremely important for laying out a pathway for career development.

- Influencing important people who may be of benefit for future business.

- Planning each step to influence concerned followers and people will always be a smart move to build more confidence.

Strategically designing the plan and transparently laying out the needed facts in front of the followers can enhance a sense of trust among the leader and the followers, which may prove to be crucial for setting a strong foundation right at the beginning.

Tactical Influence

The art of influencing the minds of others can be considered to be a profound skill that is required in almost every sphere of a person's life, and not just as a leader. The tact that is required to build an effective plan to influence others can, whatsoever, be a tad bit difficult for many.

Generally, leaders are said to use various tactics as per the need for specific objectives. There may be cases when many leaders may not just have to create an influence on their followers and subordinates; rather, there will be many occasions where they will have no other choice but to make an attempt to influence people higher in the hierarchy than them. For example, every leader will have to study the situation with caution and then go ahead with their strategy to create influence according to the set goals. Tactical influence can be used to gather support from people who are important to achieve a goal. A good leader has to figure out which type of tactic should be used to create an impactful influence. Here are some of the tactical influences that are used widely:

- Reciprocity: Any form of business requires some form of give-and-take. The reciprocity involved, and the hope that a favor will be returned in the future, is one of the tact factors that is widely used in almost every sphere of the world and business.

- Creating a bias: The psychology of human beings is such that biases are easily developed in terms of one's prejudices. Strong feelings of likings and dislikes can make or break decisions and hence, can decide the future of a business relationship as well. Almost every leader has to be liked and respected by their subordinates and peers. Then only will they be able to build an empire of their own.

- Delegated authority: By identifying the tact to influence the delegated authority, a leader can, to a large extent, indirectly control many managerial decisions made in the higher hierarchical level than him. A leader should be knowledgeable enough to create a statistical analysis of the various information related to the higher authoritative figures. By doing so, the leader can further create a situation to plan and present plans and to present oneself in a positive and likable manner. With the correct support and guidance of the experienced and senior members of the organization, a leader can flourish in one's business by learning from the experiences made by seniors, and also using their influence for further benefit.

- Calm but proactive: A calm mind can help a person think clearly and straight. This is a quality that every leader must possess. Every person does get hit with some adversity, time and again, in their personal as well as professional life. One of the biggest challenges of working as a leader can be with the role of dealing with people's issues. No two people can think and act exactly in the same manner, and understanding the mindset is a task that is not only difficult but can be equally hard-hitting for a leader. People will always turn towards their leader in cases of severe issues, and it is during times like these that the true character of a leader is revealed. Therefore, by staying calm, you can win half the battle, and the rest, you can work your way through by staying proactive and sharp. Understanding various business issues and then resolving those issues requires immense skill and determination, and that is a must for leaders.

- Excellence in the presentation: Just cultivating ideas will not work, as a leader has to not only be full of ideas and strategies, but they must be excellent at presenting their ideas and causes. They should be efficient enough to prepare a good discussion and should have exceptional oratory skills. Without verbal convincing, it can get a bit tiresome to influence the minds of the people. With proper strategy, a leader should be ready to work with diverse people, all with different mindsets. The more support leaders gain, the stronger they can rise as effective leaders.

Thus, no doubt it can be said that any team needs its planning on point. Without a solid direction, it is extremely strenuous for followers to move forward. It is all up to the leader to create a favorable situation by keeping everyone motivated and content.

Situational Influence

Situations rarely stay the same for an extended period of time. Conditions tend to change quite often, and more so in a business-based organization. The market with demand and supply changes rarely remains stagnant. It further creates a conundrum in the behavior of the people, stakeholders, and others related to the process chain. Sometimes, physical factors and other times, social factors play a significant role in creating a situation. Situational influence is a term that is most widely used in a context that is related to the market, involving buyers and sellers.

What makes leaders strike out in such a situation is their ability to influence others even when different and sometimes tough situations are also placed before them. So, how can they use their ability to influence a situation where, for example, the market is crashing down? The prime step for them would be to study the scenario in a detailed manner, from which they could effectively take part in the discussions that could help their subordinates and peers rise from the arduous situation. They have to have an in-depth knowledge of the topic or issue on which the debates and meetings are based.

It is a known fact that, in most businesses, influence is always situational. Therefore, all leaders have to learn to understand everything under the sun that is essential in the business or organization they belong to. By understanding the workplace situations, every leader can start working on the minds of the coworkers or subordinates, as they have to make sure that the motivation of the people is not shaken in any situation. Control is the most important key in influencing the audience, and that can be done by using the relative knowledge that you have of the particular subject.

Let's take a simple example of a cardiologist. He is an expert in his subject concerning any matter related to his specialty, which gives him immense confidence to easily influence his patients and people concerned with the specific subject. However, his confidence will not be as high in a field that may be owned by a dentist. The point is that situations will not always be limited to a certain type, and there will be a plethora of difficulties in the way of a leader. It is how he handles every circumstance by using tact and intellect that makes his grip on his followers much stronger. However, in simple terms, here are a few circumstances where you can use the theory of situational influence:

- Every leader should always be aware of their organization and their strengths. By doing so, they will be more confident in comparison to their peers.

- Preparation is the key! Hence, understanding the situation beforehand, and hence, preparing enough for it, can be extremely helpful in influencing the target audience.

- They should be able to push aside their agendas at the right time, and they should also be ready to back off for the overall benefit of their team.

Therefore, it can be seen that every leader has to be capable enough to use tact and their wisdom to overcome issues that may be situational.

Self-Help Influence

Influence is not just about creating a difference in someone else's mind. An individual may at times rely on a self-help strategy to overcome internal issues and develop further for the better. This is a technique that is used to understand one's agendas, and at the same time, to study one's barriers. It is but natural that with self-realization, it becomes imperative at times to let yourself take someone else's influence for improvement.

For example, with the overbearing stress caused by different situations at work and home, you often tend to get depleted of energy. It is during such a time when you often tend to look for other mediums to get yourself influenced in a positive manner. When confronted with extreme stress, one often tends to take the shelter of philosophical programs, spa sessions, relaxation programs, therapies, diet regimes, yoga classes, and exercise regimes. By taking an external medium to help yourself or rather get influenced in a manner that is beneficial for personal and professional growth, you can find manifold ways to get a fresh set of perspectives.

This concept of the self-help-based theory is an extremely tactful method that can be used not only to help build your personality as a tough leader, but will also help you understand the dynamics of the people you would want to get affected. By doing so, you can, as a leader, increase your influence in the organization, and more so by enhancing the overall productivity of the business. Self-help-based influence can be used for the following reasons:

- Self-help-based influence theory is helpful if you feel the need to upgrade your skills and hone your knowledge.

- To apply this theory into practice, you have to understand the logic and deeper meaning of how this technique works.

- By excelling in this method, you can become a leader with a reputation known for being a team player.

- Connections are easy to make when communication is done in a smooth way.

Hence, it can be seen how, by ways of getting influenced, leaders can strategically use it to influence their desired target audience effectively.

Unintended Influence

We all have heard that sometimes many things can back-fire and an entirely unexpected outcome takes place. This is a theory of an influence technique that is more about an unintended clout effect. On numerous occasions, we have all been through a situation where we try to con-vince another individual about something, but he, on the contrary, does completely the opposite. This situation, if it ever occurs in a professional environment, can have the potential to do more harm than good. Such instances can be seen more in a political scenario.

Many times, when candidates, on purpose, utter sen-tences that may further create a different situation alto-gether, such a theory can be utilized on many different occasions to fit the needs of the hour. For example, this technique can be used to push forward or cancel projects that you think have not been fair to your effort. However, when instances of pushback happen, many tweaks can be made to reallocate the resources and by changing the priority of the projects. This can be a deciding factor for you. If the authorities go ahead with the implementation of the system and convince the organizational heads, it can be a win-win situation for you. Here are a few ways in which you can use unintended influence techniques:

- Careful study of the situation that led to the hap-penings around you can later become advanta-geous for you.

- An alert mind is a mandate. You have to be conscious of the fact that situations and dynamics take no time to change. You must always be aware of what changes are taking place and how they may affect your situation or position in the organization.

Therefore, by using this remarkable technique of unintended influence, you can carve your way through to become an effective leader.

Inverted Influence

This tactic is a bit disingenuous but is considered to have proven to help individuals gain the trust and support of people on a wide scale. Time and again, there have been instances when people have used others' influence to gain more support, favor, and attention. However, there are many cases when you are left with not many choices other than to use your industry clout and to further use the authorities to influence major decisions to your advantage. Many leaders also tend to use this theory to achieve a higher rate of visibility. This method does come with a rule, and that is, this approach has to be used when necessary and that too, without causing any backlashes from the outcomes.

Reverse Influence

Haven't we heard about the concept of reverse psychology? This theory is not much different from reverse influence. This technique uses a lot of intelligence and perfect tact ideas. For example, there are numerous people who would just do something for the simple reason that someone said they could not do so in the first place.

This cannot be disregarded. It has to be counted as a form of influence. Numerous people designated for leadership and higher roles are seen to use this technique. Many times, they ask their subordinates to prove them wrong about an idea or a vision. This fact, which refuses to accept any negative statement about their caliber, is what this theory thrives on.

These were a few major influence techniques that can be used for the betterment of building a stronger perspective and persona of a leader.

Communicate with influence

Not just communication, effective communication is the need of the hour for any leader. With the increase in the complexity of the business environment, the need for advanced communication for purposes of setting internal organization structure, managing external collaborations, and leading crucial business goals has all but increased.

There are numerous qualities that every leader must possess to become a leader who can influence their followers, but the one factor that tops them all is the skill to communicate effectively with others. It is a core business strength that can give an added weightage to any deal.

In the hardcore setup and business modules of today, a great challenge that has the potential to create a massive conundrum for a leader is to choose a particular way of communicating with the rest. Different factors like psychological, geographical, cultural, habitual, and even political factors play a major role in making it all the more difficult task for a leader to understand the most effective means of communication based on a given circumstance.

For example, there has recently been an influx of massive globalization effects in the aspect of work culture. Numerous teams and employees are working from remote areas, which can be not just far-off locations but also locations that are oceans apart. Therefore, it is a challenge for a leader to place his trust and effort on employees who may be from a completely different continent, for that matter. In a situation like this, the only factor that can solve such difficulties is by adopting a means of a structured communication path.

A very interesting post in Forbes, written by G. Riley Mills, the co-author of the widely acclaimed book "The Pin Drop Principle", has laid out a list of five C's that should be incorporated by every leader to influence a listener or an audience. Let us just look into it in a bit more detail:

The 5 C's Theory of Communication

Have we ever thought about the reasons that make a leader or a public figure mostly stand out from the rest? As we have already mentioned, it is not always about the position and the hierarchy. It is how a leader should be a great communicator. Leaders are already elevated to a position where they can influence a reform, whether it is political, social, cultural, or even organizational. What is the use of the platform given, if not utilized in a manner to spread a positive influence on the followers? How can you make a difference when you enter a room full of your competitors? It is your skill as a communicator that has the potential to roll the dice in your favor in most situations.

Magnanimous figures who have brought substantial changes in the plot of history and time, like Winston

Churchill, Ronald Reagan, Henry Ford, John Wooden, Billy Graham, Oprah Winfrey, and Barack Obama, are all said to be great communicators. With their strong opinions and very rightly applied deeds in their respective fields, they have all made noteworthy efforts to bring about a shift in public opinion and their reaction. If we take examples of figures we all have witnessed in recent times, then we can name Barack Obama, who is a phenomenal speaker and communicator. He simply did not rule over the hearts of many, but equally became an inspiration for people all around the globe. You can even take the example of Stephen Colbert, who is an exceptionally brilliant communicator. He has the ability to strike a rapport with a large section of people who follow his witty and humorous talks that not only entertain but successfully make numerous cultural and political references.

The main idea is how and what the ways are to make your thoughts, ideas, and actions as a leader resonate with the people and followers. Here are the five C's that you can utilize to improve your ability to influence your audience, listeners, or followers:

- Clear: As a leader, it is your job to make yourself heard and understood by your followers. This is because you cannot expect to get support and loyalty from the rest if there is no clarity of reasoning. According to a study mentioned in an article in Forbes, around 46% of people remain unclear about the agenda of the meeting even at the end. Clarity is the defining factor. You have to be crisp and precise while at the same time firmly presenting your ideas and visions to the rest of the group. Any form of message that you deliver concerning the objectives and goals of the organization, you as a leader have to make sure that you are articulate enough to be understood clearly by the rest of the people. Furthermore, make sure that the presentations and the mediums that you arrange for any such meeting address all the points that are needed to establish a clear-cut connection with the rest.

- Concise: The most remarkable example of this is the noted speech by Abraham Lincoln given at the Gettysburg Address. This speech is considered one of the most effective speeches in the history of time, lasting only three minutes. Isn't it breathtaking to imagine the impact of this speech of just 272 words? If we look into most of our work scenarios, there are plenty of meetings and conferences held regularly to cover issues that could have just been written and sent in a simple email. The crux is that wasting the time of the people just to prove a point is something a leader should avoid doing. People tend to lose interest after a certain time. Therefore, the shorter and smarter your speech is, the more influence you are bound to have on the minds of people.

- Confidence: The attitude by which a person pitches his ideas is what makes a leader. Nobody would ever want a leader who they could never look up to. Hence, as a leader, it is pertinent that you ooze confidence from your overall persona. It is a fact that everyone can get jitters of nervousness, but if the followers sense even a slight bit of nervousness in the speech and body language of the leader, then that can lead to serious repercussions. Always make sure to have a posture and body language that is relaxed and strong. Instability in behavior and the expression of ideas can create massive problems. Be confident throughout your addressing of the people and also interacting with the people, making your presence felt firmly and confidently. Confidence can be extremely reassuring and can make any individual feel safe and secure about their identity and purpose in life.

- Credible: Trust is always earned through credibility, and this is of utmost importance in leadership qualities. Any business is built on the foundation of trust, and if any of your partners or coworkers do not find you sincere, then that can raise issues in terms of business outcomes. It is a business process wherein a solid base has to be formed consisting of mutual trust and confidence with the potential client. Make sure to prepare before any form of interaction or meeting with a potential client. Be aware of their business structure and conditions. A good communicator has to make sure that he is vocal about every aspect that may be beneficial for the business. With the right words pointed at the legitimate clauses and workings of the business, a leader can prove his eminence. When dealing with clients, avoid hedging words like "kind of" as well as verbal infections like "hmms," "uh," "ah," and the like. A reputation for credibility can help any person weigh in more than anyone else without it.

- Compelling: With good persuasion ability, a leader can influence his audience in any situation. As a leader, you have to capture the minds of the people by using the three main means of persuasion technique as defined by Aristotle. People lean towards a speaker or a leader who appears to be honest, believable, and with whom they feel a connection.

Several leaders make an effort to communicate only when they feel it is OK for them. This is not a very correct approach because to succeed in a matrix organization, communication needs to be more deliberate and all parties involved in the communication process must be taken into consideration. A strategically laid out coordination plan is what is required to make the communication flow natural and on point in any given situation. Successful projects need a communication layout, which clearly outlines who has certain information, who needs certain information, when they need it and where to find it. Furthermore, in the present era, work modules have changed to an advanced level. Most of the connections happen through virtual corridors. Hence, make sure to accept and embrace technology and utilize it to upgrade your business and hone your skills. Learn all the technological tools to improve your communication game. The point is that you have to understand the vitality of effective communication to become a leader who has a great influence on people.

4

Influencing Change

Since the time of the inception of civilization, one factor that has marked its way to remain the most constant is 'change'. It is indeed an irony that something as fickle and in motion as 'change' has remained the most permanent. History has witnessed a continuous process of change in almost every field possible. Change can be caused due to internal or external factors, both of which depend on the circumstance and the classification of the changing structure. Sometimes, just a mere push is made, and reform takes place, and sometimes immense effort and compromises are needed to bring about an effective change. Due to several reasons like these, change management can be a process that may prove to be a heavy burden on the role of a leader. Nevertheless, every leader can be an effective change agent if they use their power to influence others precisely.

On a personal level, have you ever tried to make even a slight change at your office or any place where you work? The change may be, for instance, influencing the behavior of a colleague, creating a rift in relationships at work, bringing a change in the work culture, etc. Have you ever tried to persuade your loved ones to behave in a way that you desire, even in a private setting? All these complex questions lead to a simple answer: Yes. It may be a case when you have not directly tried to bring any such change, but at some point in time, we all have tried to influence someone's mind as per our wishes. It may be as simple as influencing your friend to try the new popcorn flavor that you have longed to have for a long time, or maybe love the most. Thus, the part of the influence in our day-to-day lives cannot be overruled in any way, and not at all in the case of an individual who has aspirations to become a leader looked upon by all.

A task that is of utmost significance to a leader's role is to bring triumphant outcomes even during times of uncertainty. Many people have an innate talent for influencing others, but this does not imply that a person without a natural flair for influencing others cannot hone their talent to influence their surrounding environment. You can improve this skill by observing the following core points:

- Understand the tact to 'nudge' in the process of decision-making.

- Enhance your skill of persuasion without making it appear like manipulation.

- Investigate your strengths and weaknesses and ask for feedback from people who matter. Do not waste time but start working on them right away.

- Do not have a one-track mind; be open to suggestions no matter how critical they may be.

- Give your best to be adaptable in a variety of circumstances.

- Make an effort to shift mindsets across the organization and, specifically, the team that you belong to.

There is a high probability that most people who have had their share of experience in any organization, governmental or non-governmental, have been witness to the change in dynamics of the team and the organization with the change of leaders. The leadership role is critical in binding or breaking the scenario of any workplace. Unfortunately, such situations are seen quite often in an organizational setup. However, it is not always the change of the leader that causes problems. It is the type of leadership that is considered to be more impactful. As a result, whether a leader is new or experienced, one factor that they must always be careful about is having a positive influence on the behavior and lives of those who follow them. No doubt, leaders have to be role models for bringing in reforms that will help in bringing diverse reforms for the benefit of the people.

How to Bring Positive Change in Your Life

Any change that you want to see should, in the first place, start from within you. As a leader who intends to move forward by keeping the perspectives of the followers in place, you must never forget that it is you who should believe in the reforms that you plan to levy on others. Influence is a change that is supposed to be brought into place without letting it look like a form of manipulation or a tactful stance.

Humans, by nature, are not very welcoming to any sudden changes in any aspect of their lives. Resistance is what follows if a solid justification is not provided for any new change that is thrown at them. Therefore, as a leader who is empathetic at the same time, you must take a few considerations before taking the relevant strategies to bring any change. First and foremost, look for ways to help you, as an individual, rather than just as a leader, make positive changes in your personal and professional life. Here are a few tips that could help you make positive changes in your life:

- Identify what you want to change: Every leader has to have a clear sense of what their vision is all about. Before taking a step towards starting a change program, they must make sure that there is not an iota of doubt in their mind about their work or their strategies. According to Anthony Grant, an associate professor from the University of Sydney's Coaching Psychology Unit, "You need to be able to identify what it is about the goal that adds to you as a person, that makes you feel better and more expansive." This theory is based on the logic that if your objectives are in sync with your core values, then there will be a high probability of positive outcomes.

- Avoid negativity: Surround yourself with people who add positive energy to your personality, so do not let the negativity of a person or their thoughts influence your peace of mind in any way. The fast-paced life that most of us lead has not only given us numerous opportunities to achieve our dreams but has, at the same time, brought substantial pressure, resulting in exhaustion and stress. Such circumstances can not only hamper our professional lives, but can equally deteriorate our mental and physical health. Therefore, one of the best ways to attract positivity is by avoiding anything or anyone with a negative vibe. The more you focus on the pros of a situation, the more you will be able to solve the cons.

- Be kind and empathetic: Acts of kindness and feelings of empathy have only good outcomes to offer. Understandably, the workspace often becomes a place for hardcore competition, and in such a case, it becomes difficult to always think with your heart. However, you can make small changes, like asking your peers and subordinates if they are facing any difficulty in doing any task. You could make a simple gesture like offering your colleague a glass of water or maybe a cup of coffee while coming from the cafeteria. On a personal level, you could delve deeper and see where you can make amends to better your relationship with someone, be it, friends or family. Even the tiniest of gestures can help you grow as a person, and especially a leader with qualities of kindness and empathy can turn out to be a real gem.

- Build a support system: We are all social beings, and thriving alone can be said to be a tad bit unrealistic. Every individual requires a strong support system, be it friends, family, colleagues, or any positive relationship. There will be a point in life when support will be required, and people we choose to rely on during difficult times become our guides in the long run. Therefore, always have a set of people to back you up and give you a feeling of self-worth when you need it the most.

- Take one step at a time: Taking a tiny step is way more convenient than taking a big leap. Small steps towards achieving your goals can be manageable and less complicated than taking a step with a higher impact. Do not rush and take your time to make the correct impact, rather than jumping on an action that may dampen your image to a certain extent.

- Develop habits to calm your mind: Our daily habits are what groom our overall personality. Small changes in your regular lifestyle can have a more positive influence on your mind and body. Regular exercise, healthy eating, practicing yoga, meditation, and the like can help boost mental and physical health. By incorporating habits like these, you will feel good about yourself. Anxiety and stress will also be reduced substantially, which will eventually help boost your confidence.

Therefore, it can be seen that positive influence has to start with yourself. You have to make sure to incorporate all the positive vibes within yourself before going out and encouraging the same from others. By tweaking here and there, you could bring more security, confidence, and happiness to yourself, which will benefit your professional life as well.

How to Influence Change in Others

Recent years have seen an exponential speed in terms of professional growth. The way a person manages their professional life along with their personal life is exasperating to even imagine because the perseverance that is required to maintain it can be extremely arduous. In a time like this, a leader's role is to act as a change leader and influence a change, which is a task that can be highly challenging.

The reason why the popularity of the concept of change management and change agents has risen over the years is that, in any form of business, the main goal is to succeed and gain the top spot. The only way an organization can mark its place at the highest level is by doing something different and worthwhile than the rest of the competitors.

Furthermore, this comes along with other challenges. For example, the typical mindset of a large number of people is that they will choose something they already feel secure about rather than venture into something that is said to be better. As a leader who is keen on influencing and bringing a solution to such problems, you must make sure to present them with all the positive reasons why such new changes should be made. For example, when mobile phones with cameras were introduced, there was a large section of people all around the world who thought that it was not a good idea to have a phone with a camera. This chain of thought arose from many instances of people hearing about how the internet and easy access to it through phones can have a horrible impact on the minds of people, especially the young ones. As a business leader dealing with this arena, in this case, the first step you should take is to address a wide section of the people through meetings, conferences, advertisements, writings, etc. It is your job to tap into their thoughts and help them make a wise decision by accepting a modern device. By projecting the pros and cons of the usage of a camera phone, you can very tactfully persuade them to buy the product that you intend to make useful.

The process of bringing others to change themselves or accept a new method of change sounds easy in theory but can be a laborious task. To simplify the steps, here are a few ways in which you can influence change in others:

- Let the other person talk first about their problems and overall perspective. Listening to their point of view can be an extremely beneficial mode of conduct, as it will build up a feeling of trust.

- Be authentic in your approach, as the core of building a strong relationship is based on interactions that are genuine and not manipulative. When people start believing in your ideas and you as a person then, they will be less likely to doubt your theories.

- After you lay the foundation of trust and authenticity, strike the deal. Layout your plans about bringing new changes in the system and them as individuals. With proper persuasion, you will be able to influence them positively.

- Clarify all their doubts and questions. Show them the strategic plans and how you intend them to work. Having a transparent understanding of the people will help you gain more access to their thoughts and actions.

Once you have researched thoroughly about the subject and have made a sincere effort to study the perspective of the people concerned, you will be able to lead the way towards greater success with the support of the overall team, the people, and the overall organization.

Positively Influence Change at Work

We all talk about issues and the different ways to resolve them. Most leaders, all the more, are placed on a pedestal where they are bound by their role to bring about significant changes that can improve the prospects of the organization they are involved with. Therefore, they have to choose the best possible influence tactic that will suit the situation. Here are a few techniques by which leaders can up their game to influence others, especially at a workspace:

- Analyze the situation: Be aware of the reasons why you are vested in a particular job and how important are the outcomes for you. As a leader, you must be certain about why you need to influence some people, and then accordingly, set your strategies to work towards that direction.

- Target audience: A sound understanding of the audience that you mean to reach is essential for a strategy of influence to work smoothly. A wider understanding of the perspectives of different people involved in the work process is needed for any leader to work without forming any conflict of interests.

- Understand your stakeholders: Many of an organization's decisions are based on the interest of the stakeholders. There will always be a high probability of them having different opinions, interests, priorities, and agendas. You will have to come to a conclusion about how to influence each stakeholder as per their requirement and personalities. Accordingly, a leader must set plans to influence them as subtly as possible. Make a careful study of every individual's role and contribution in the organization, and then go ahead with further making goals.

- Self-evaluate your abilities: Always come to terms with yourself. Take a deep and honest analysis of your skills and techniques of working. By doing so, you will be able to understand what holds you down and what strengths take you up. Think about what tactics have been useful and have given the best results in the past. Collaborate with your peers and subordinates and try to get occasional feedback for them. By being rational, you can take a healthy step in working towards your goal of creating an influence on your target people.

Leadership influence has the potential of bringing massive changes in an organization. Any workplace with a large number of people is bound to have an amalgamation of opinions and work styles. In order to bring about a vital change, a leader has to create influence without any apparent effort. Most importantly, it is image and reputation that will inspire the people to follow them.

A riveting incident mentioned in an article in the "Change Folio" about Apple's founder Steve Jobs, is a great example of how the influence of a leader works at his workplace. There was an instance where the developers of Apple's team presented the iPod's prototype to Steve Jobs. He lifted it, weighed it in his hands, and on the spot rejected it, saying it was too big. The developers and engineers who had worked on that device were disappointed and tried to explain how difficult it would be to reduce the size. Steve Jobs stayed silent and listened, then he went and dropped the device in the fish tank. No sooner did the device reach the bottom of the tank than bubbles started to ooze out of the device. He then said that those were air bubbles, which meant that there was space inside the device that could have been reduced in size.

This is a clear example of how Steve Jobs was a leader who was not only inspirational but at the same time had the skill to influence the thought processes of people. Leaders indeed have a tremendous role to play in influencing the behaviors of others, be it positive as well as negative.

When it comes to employees and organizations, there is a huge onset of rapid development which brings along with it massive changes in technology and methodologies. One of the biggest challenges of a leadership role is to deal with resistance and people's issues. Leaders are always kept on close vigil by the rest of the people, as they are looked upon as a source of inspiration, hope, guidance, and support. Heavy eyes of scrutiny will always befall them. They have to be agile and be a part of the change management process without causing damage to their repute and vision. Here are a few ways in which a leader can help bring positive influence to the workplace:

- Help people understand the value of change: Resistance is one of the most common reactions when a new reform is introduced without much announcement in the first place. In such a case, what can make people accept change? Value is the answer. It is true that humans work on the basis of a give and take relationship. With the same logic, a person will not invest their energy in something that they do not see as being of any value. As a leader, you have to tap into this psychology to influence the minds of the people. You will have to make them understand the value that a new change will bring to their lives for the better. By taking action like this, you will slowly but surely see a big rise in the number of your audience.

- Face the resistance: To solve any problem, one should first accept the existence of an issue. It is only after an issue is acknowledged that a solution can be sought. As a leader, you should observe every ounce of voice coming from the people. Listen to them, hear out their concerns, face all the reasons for their resistance to change. Encourage the people and influence their minds to make a positive decision rather than just causing a stumbling block on every new change that is introduced by the leadership.

- Be on point: It is quite evident that people will be in a state of a conundrum with any sudden change. A leader has to clarify any doubts or misconceptions regarding the same. Be on point and do not use terms and phrases that could lead to more confusion. Be mindful of how and what important details you provide to people.

- Be engaging: Communicate with your audience with clarity and be approachable to a certain extent. Create an ambiance at the workplace where people feel free to communicate and get more engaged in productive activities. As a leader, it would be wise to get engaged in team management meetings and other programs at the workplace. It is a motivational sight for the rest of the team members to see the leader engrossed in the numerous team management programs. This gives a sense of consistent trust, which can influence the minds of people in the most positive manner.

By adapting to the various scenarios at the professional level, leaders have to prove themselves to be inspirational role models for the rest of the people. By doing so, they can not only inspire others and bring positive influence to the workplace but can successfully influence the minds of the people to think and act in the manner that is required for the benefit of the overall vision of the organization.

5

How to Persuade and Influence

To believe that you've never made a decision based on an irrational thought can be quite tricky. Even for the most practical people on the planet, claiming that no amount of influence has clouded their thoughts or actions in the past or will do so in the future is a near-impossible answer. This puts us at a crossroads in which we must comprehend how persuasion and influence work. As a leader, it is your caliber that counts, your potential to achieve a goal and get things done in the way that is needed. Your success is often measured by the challenges that you face and have come out of as a big success.

Survival is the key in every sphere of life in this world, and no doubt, doing so with victory is what a person with leadership qualities must aim for. However, the path towards triumph is a steep way up. It may lead to many falls, but one factor that will help clear out the road is the art of persuasion. Similarly, influence has a big part to play in framing the minds of people and in getting returns that may be successful. However, what is the actual difference between persuasion and influence? Let us dive into the intricacies of the two highly effective terms:

Persuasion Versus Influence

Let's take a pause and think about the basic difference that you feel is between persuasion and influence. Can we think of the areas where these two tactics strike out separately in dealing with an issue and in getting a job done? Furthermore, it can be said that there is a thin line that separates these two types of methods that are used widely by leaders.

Persuasion is a method of presenting a case and taking it to a point to move people to a point where they agree. Influence is more tactful in approach. It is how a situation is molded to manipulate the perspective of the people concerned. These two terms have a high chance of being utilized interchangeably, and more so, they do not make a disastrous difference at all. Persuasion and leadership are two important skills that make a critical difference in the style and quality of a leader.

Persuasion is more about putting forward an effort to convince another person to do something you want them to. Whereas, to influence someone requires more skill and can be innate in many individuals. Leadership is about dealing with a group of people with basic emotions who are diverse in various aspects. One of the most interesting theories about the power of influence is how rational persuasion works. Let's get into the deeper understanding of aspects, such as these:

Rational Persuasion

Power can be subjective on many levels. It can be based on an individual's perception of their skill at influencing events around them, be it social or political. It can come in countless forms, from a hierarchical basis or on a personal level of power to influence others. As we have already discussed, the different patterns of influence like consultation, collaboration, inspiration, and the like. However, in all of these different influence techniques, rational persuasion stands out to be a great method.

If you are a leader heading a group of people or a team at your organization, rational persuasion can help you in your effort to influence the people around you. It is a simple method that is used by amalgamating the request of approach with arguments that are extremely rational in nature. The request made is in the form of a pressured appeal, but the arguments used in the process are backed with factual evidence. Due to the reasons that are justified in the most practical ways, the request that is made is proved to be feasible.

Many leaders who follow a rational persuasion method to build their influence over the minds of the people they work with are often looked upon as someone who talks on point and is considered super objective and relevant. Many times, such leaders follow a prototype process in which they make strategies to convince their concerned audience to accept decisions and new changes. They execute their plans by using mediums of charts, statistics, graphs, picture proofs, surveys, snippets from people's statements, etc. By doing so, they explain their point and succeed in justifying their position. In a very subtle way, they make it clear that a leader's perspective is the most justifiable and rational.

Major analysis, expert knowledge, and experience are used in preparing a statistical chart that is presented to the audience. They often cite reasons that talk about the benefits that the new scheme or a project will bring in people's professional and personal lives. They never go off track and talk about data analysis by presenting the details of the surveys done or the given data details. This type of persuasion method usually follows the top-down direction of approach in the case of hierarchy; it has hardly any scope of being followed in a bottom to top-level path.

Rational persuasion is based on a work value that does not make any threats or misuse any power of any person involved. It is as simple as any process can get because what most leaders do in such a situation is that they put forward their opinions, ideas, and strategies in front of the people concerned. There is no speck of ingratiating themselves to the other members of the organization as all their discussions are based on nothing but logic and excellently explained ideas that offer the best option for the given circumstance.

Key Concepts

Leaders are always under the close watch of the people in general. In such a scenario, they cannot afford to make a blunder and lose the chance given to them by their position to go ahead and influence a large audience. The unforgettable speech "I Have a Dream" by Martin Luther King, Jr. and "Greed is Good" in the film Wall Street by Gordon Gekko have both managed to garner magnanimous success in influencing a large number of people from all over the globe. These two magnanimous figures were not just good at oratory skills, but it was their speeches that were based on a logic that garnered them more respect and followers.

We all, at one point of time in our lives, have been influenced by consultation and inspirational programs. Influence needs a solid foundation of persuasion technique, and the leaders mainly need to be absolutely genuine about their approach and goals. As a leader, you ought to make sure that all the facts that are presented to the audience are relevant and true to their claims, or else, as fast as a person can gain attention, doubly fast it can be given up by their followers. By keeping your facts straight, you will keep misinformation and misunderstandings at bay for a long period of time. The reason why so much stress is laid on genuinely is that a leader must gain the trust of the rest of the people. If there is even an iota of doubt or dishonesty seen from a leader's face, there is a high chance of risking the support of the followers in the long run as well. You will not only lose support but will not be able to gain a perfect buy-in for your ideas even in the following days.

The main concept that should be followed by each leader at all times is to have a broad knowledge of the subject. Only by doing so, will they be able to set their facts straight and present a valid argument to appeal to their peers, subordinates, and followers. Any claims that turn out to be false at the end of the deal may result in a significant loss of followers in the long run. Trust is a big word, and any form of business would struggle to thrive without it. Therefore, as a leader, it is your prerogative to build a connection with the audience based on trust and respect.

In "Decoding Inspirational Leadership", Claudio Fesser, the writer, points out that statements made by leaders have the potential of leaving a strong impact on the minds of their audience. He gives examples of certain statements used frequently by leaders while using rational persuasion, such as: "The company's transformation is necessary to achieve growth, to reduce costs, and to beat the competition.", "I want you to take action.", "Given the data available, the most logical approach is...", and the like.

Therefore, it is quite clear how logic with supportive evidence works in making rational decisions. Rational leaders are more on the safer side, as they have all their actions backed up by intellect and careful planning.

Effects of Rational Persuasion

Change is not easily welcomed by most people. It is natural to not feel comfortable adapting to something new.

The replacements and the confusion caused by matters of change in professional and personal spheres can have an unimaginable impact on the minds and lives of people, and these impacts may all be different for every individual. The confusion that is created due to such scenarios is said to be controlled by leaders through the usage of rational persuasion methods.

If you are a leader, the first step that you must always take when given responsibility of great power is to understand and study the field that you are put in with extra dedication. With correct reasons in place, any argument that vouches to bring any form of resistance that may hamper any operation of the organization can be countered by a rational debate from the side of the leader. With meta-cognition, mindful research, and practical persuasion, a leader can no doubt create a strong argument, even at the toughest times.

Rational persuasion can help you win a bid or make your pitch argument much stronger. No wonder this form of persuasion technique is often confused with manipulation. However, it is very different. Using debates and discussions, stating all the pros and cons of a subject matter, and even laying out the strategic plans with full analysis can help the audience decide how the ideas laid out by the leader are much more authentic and feasible. Manipulation, if you must say, but not with a negative connotation.

The primary purpose of rational persuasion is to make your ideas the ideas of everyone else at the end. It is very important to set aside your egos and not think of taking credit for every piece of work that you do. There will come a time when there might be differences of opinions between the team members, but it is all up to the attitude of the leader that will help settle any form of an issue by using a rational method like this.

Emotional Persuasion

One must think twice, or rather several times, before claiming that they have never let their emotions impact their decision-making and have always stayed true only to rational thinking. The fact is that we all, at some point in our lives, have or will in the future, get triggered by certain emotions and that, in turn, may have an effect on our professional circumstances. Emotions play a role that is highly important in the process of persuasion and, in the end, in influencing the minds of others. This is the very reason why emotional persuasion has a higher potential to lead to conversion.

Shanelle Mullin, in her article called "Emotional Persuasion: The Advanced Guide", writes about how emotion has a huge part to play in persuasion. In her article, she discusses how a renowned neurologist, Antonio Damasio, experimented with the effects of emotion on aspects of decision-making. It is intriguing to know that he based his study on people who had brain damage and were incapable of feeling any emotion. To understand conversion optimization, one must understand how this study went forward. All the candidates for the study behaved normally. However, one thing that struck out was that these people were found to be incapable of making any decisions, even simple decisions like what food to eat and what clothes to wear.

The brain is also responsible for the formation of different emotions. There are two sides to the neural system. The left side is linked with emotions like pride, anger, and happiness. Whereas the right side of the brain is linked with emotions like fear, disgust, and avoidance. It is often referred to as dual processing in the field of psychology. As per this psychological theory, it is believed that the two systems of the brain are also called system one and system two, the first is associated with the unconscious, automatic, low effort, and fast, whereas the latter is associated with conscious, controlled, high effort, and slow characteristics. In plain words, it can be said that system one of our brains is responsible for our logical behavior, and system two is responsible for the emotional decisions that we make, but it also tends to rationalize those thoughts later with time.

It has been observed that emotional persuasion receives more success on the road towards conversion. Simple examples based on buying impulses can be taken to state how emotions drive a person to consume something without rationalizing it first. Advertisement agencies can vouch for this. Most of the ads that we see focus on how emotionally we connect with the thought of buying a product. If you analyze numerous winning advertising campaigns, then you will be able to understand how emotional triggers are used to sell an idea or a product. Take the example of the brand TOMS shoes, as this is a brand that is known for the social cause that it is connected with. When you buy a pair of TOMs shoes, the brand vouches that they donate a pair of shoes to an underprivileged child. The philanthropic emotion that is attached to this brand is what connects and stays in the minds of the consumers. As much as the brand is doing a fabulous job of helping children in need, it cannot also be denied from a consumer's perspective that the overwhelming emotions triggered by thinking about a noteworthy cause is remarkable.

Therefore, it can be said that emotional persuasion can be used in countless ways. Paying attention to the needs of others and, accordingly, getting attention can be a tact that can help in many ways, laying the foundation of emotional persuasion.

The Persuasive Leader

Persuasive leadership is a style in which the opinions of the people are listened to, and decisions are made to set goals while keeping in mind the general satisfaction of the people. This is a method that includes participation, delegative, collaborative, and, interestingly, the Laissez-faire methods. However, these methods have their ways of working. Persuasion, in simple words, is the main source of all these methods, as they deal with more than one person's desire to bring a decision on mutual terms.

Now, jumping straight to the point, let us discuss what the various ways in which you can become a persuasive leader are:

- Prepare the way: As a leader, you have to get your agendas straight and work on strategies to turn your visions into reality. You must understand the importance of persuading people to work as per your needs. Be aware of the fact that people do not like to be persuaded directly. Forceful persuasion may lead to opposition and polarization. Be open to dialogue and feedback, and use it to improve the situation.

- Establish credibility: Genuine behavior is expected from a leader. Every leader who can be trusted with their words is the one that will be able to persuade and sway the minds of the people on their side with ease. Be clear and honest about your opinions, and refrain from appearing scheming and manipulative.

- Understand the audience: A leader has to deal with a diverse range of people and places. You will not be able to predict what kind of encounters you will have in the near future on the journey of being a leader. Study and gain knowledge about the people you are dealing with. Make sure not to offend and hurt their sentiments. Only by understanding the nature of the audience will a leader be able to persuade them.

- Do what is right: On the way towards the goal, compromises will befall us in every nook and corner of the road. You will have to face the challenges with grit and determination, and accordingly, think about all the aspects of the situation. Only with proper scrutiny of the situation will you be able to take the rightful decision. By not being prejudiced and biased, a leader will be able to make sound decisions that will prove beneficial for the present as well as the future.

- Avoid personal agendas: No leader should bring their personal agendas and ego on the path towards achieving the collective goals. By bringing personal motives in between, there will be a risk of your image being portrayed as a self-centered and egoistic leader. This can very much negate the main objective of influencing people. Instead, it will lead to a focus on your negative traits.

- Use enticing language: Great oratory skills can capture the attention of the audience. Talk with clarity and make your arguments crisp and gripping. Without holding the attention of your audience, you will not be able to persuade them to do something.

- Provide evidence: Leaders are not expected to talk without proper research and details about any matter that they address. All their arguments and debates must be supported with evidence like data, graphs, charts, etc. By presenting correct data, you can prove to the audience your authentic and professional behavior.

- Be relatable: It is difficult to persuade anyone who cannot relate to you in any manner. As a leader, you should know about what triggers the emotional attachment of the audience, tap on those emotions and make them understand your perspective, which may benefit them in the future.

Hence, we have seen how persuasion and the various types of it are quite different than just influence. Though at times, it becomes almost impossible to break a distinction between these two methods, it can be said that it is not wrong for a leader to use these two methods interchangeably at times to achieve a positive goal.

6

Consultation and Collaborative Approach in Leadership

Consultation and Collaboration are two such words that form the crux of any organization that has the foundation of respect for all categories of the workforce. Both are influencing tactics used by leaders to influence their audience.

The reason why both these factors are elusive is that in the competitive world of today, not many co-workers agree to collaborate with each other regularly. They are more concerned with competing, and sometimes too aggressively. Due to such turf at the professional front, many feel a sense of exhaustion that eventually leads to some adverse effect on general productivity. More so, a closer look at what these two methods are all about can be beneficial.

Consultation: An Influencing Tactic

Consultation is used as a tactic in many ways to create influence. In simple words, it means a source other than the leader is asked to help in influencing another group of people. The consulting industry is thriving, and its relevance is growing by the day. More and more people and companies are looking for ways to improve their organizations by enlisting the expertise of experts. It is widely seen that consultation is a method that is used

mostly in organizations that have respect for everyone's opinion, more so has a value for decision-making democratically.

We often see in the cases of corporations, and even in several governmental departments, there are a huge number of people recruited and appointed as consultants. Out of these many employees, there are a few who act as advisors to the leaders and help them in the decision-making processes. The majority of these people are nominated internally for the position, and an experienced consultant is frequently hired to work on the same. Consultants, like change agents, are typically tasked with pitching fresh ideas and effective techniques in order to get the flow toward the established objectives moving at a rapid and seamless pace.

Consultation is an effective tool that is used by numerous companies to boost their brand value. It is considered to be an interpersonal method that has the potential to address and solve a plethora of work-related issues. However, consultation is not just about giving advice and persuading people to follow a certain direction, but rather can be looked upon as an opportunity to work in collaboration with the leader and the followers without any bias. Numerous workplaces also consider consultation as a legal requirement that is much needed for a healthy and safe work environment. With debates and discussions that are studied by consultation experts, it becomes convenient for a leader to identify the potential causes of resistance and the general mindset of the workers. Therefore, consultation can be termed as an effective method of persuasion that works as per the guideline principles of persuasion and influence.

Why Collaboration Matters

Collaboration is essential in managing the leader and follower bond or any regular employer and employee dynamic. Collaboration can only be found in a space that has people who respect and are ready to listen to each other. It is a practice that helps members of an organization work together as a team, even with varied challenges. This management practice brings together the perspectives of all those involved with the team and its work in order to benefit the organization.

Recent times have seen a surge in the implementation of this method by managers of different organizations across various sectors. It is a theory, or rather a style, that does not follow the conservative top-down channel of the hierarchical structure. It challenges the very notion of the higher authorities making decisions for every spectrum of the organization without even taking any insight from the people. This approach creates a sense of unity among the managers and their coworkers, which prepares the ground for making smooth business decisions. It involves strategic business processes by keeping the core values of the company in high regard. With the practice of collaboration, the managers and the leaders themselves inspire the rest of the workers to work in a similar manner. By setting ground rules of how and what should be followed to be able to collaborate and work, the leaders demonstrate through their actions. This is keenly observed by the numerous other employees, and naturally, they collectively develop the habit of doing the same.

Any leadership program, it is said, begins with the leader, and it is up to him or her to steer it toward success or to build future blockheads through attitude and ego issues.

By embodying the work ethics and working along with the rest of the team, a leader can create an ambiance of security and togetherness for all the other members of the organization. The transparency that he uses to foster the needs of the situation can bring about a sense of trust among the others.

Collaboration is all about sharing and listening to all the different opinions involved in making the best decision for the team. The leaders who follow this approach make sure to make the environment comfortable and safe enough for the employees to open up and voice their honest thoughts and ideas across the table. It is only through ways of working together with people belonging to different backgrounds and skills that one can achieve a global outlook and diverse knowledge.

This is not only an innovative process, but many studies have proven over the years that a positive atmosphere in the workplace is capable of increasing productivity. According to Forbes, employees who are recognized and promoted are likely to have higher performance. Therefore, it can be seen how with correct collaboration, a leader can implement numerous decisions for the benefit of the overall team and yet, not encounter resistance of any sort.

Increase Your Collaborative Influence

Collaborative influence is a tactic that requires a lot of agile strategies. All leaders who intend to follow this method have to base their actions first on understanding the motivational level of the audience. They have to make sure what the trigger points are that affect the thought processes of the rest of the people on their team. Here are a few such tactics that can be used to generate collaborative influence:

- Observe the level of motivation in the audience. Motivation can be generally divided into three approaches that are based on sensation, anticipation, and social belonging. Make an effort to see on what basis the audience is feeling attached to the new change or what exactly the causes are that are making them create resistance.

- Learn the problem and then solve the issue. Consider the requirements of the people before setting new strategic goals. Take their review in a timely manner. By doing so, you will make them feel that their opinion matters and is taken into huge consideration.

- Appreciate individual strengths and accept the fact that an organization can work at its best only when an entire lot of the employees use their skills to produce a fruitful outcome. A company can never be run by the leader alone; it requires collaboration to increase its workforce. Only by leveraging on the skills of the entire lot will the organization start to prosper.

- Encourage digital collaboration to break down many metaphorical and physical obstacles affecting employees. With the collaboration of digital devices, teams can find an efficient way to get their jobs done. An influx of digital technologies can overcome the barriers that may be caused due to the remote working and unavailability of employees on many occasions. Video conferencing, team chat windows, and instant messaging can all help to make communication more efficient and effective.

Digital communication tools like Google's G-Suite are in high demand as it makes functions like the creation of files, editing, and sending it to the team much more convenient than the old practices that require time and patience.

- A leader must set a tone of collaboration by being direct about his or her intentions. A leader should always be prepared to be attacked by questions and doubts. Make sure that you never let the collaborative outlook get impacted adversely. Instead, reach a point through discussion to bring about resolutions to deal with the issues.

- Making a list of problems that need the attention of the leadership is a must to bring any form of change. The problems may not always be directly seen, but it is the job of the leader to delve deeper into the underlying causes of resistance.

- A leader should always be prepared with a contingency plan. You should always have a Plan B as a backup in case Plan A fails. Work together with the rest of the team to come to a solution that sees the interest of all the parties concerned.

- Carefully evaluate all the areas where full collaboration will be possible and can lead to profitable possibilities in the future. Always make sure to narrow down the solution options to further commit to a plan by verifying the compliance.

Hence, it can be seen that with tactful usage of collaborative leadership techniques, you can not just set goals and achieve them easily, but most importantly, it creates an ambiance that is based on mutual trust and honesty, and that is what helps in building strong relationships.

Collaborative Leadership

The power of unity cannot be underestimated on any level, and by embracing this positive factor, a leader can take the organization through leaps and bounds towards a place of success. By using strategic thinking, communication, and empathy, the leader can help hone the practical skills of the employees. Collaboration is believed to empower the voices of people, and collaborative leaders work responsibly towards development as a whole because, with a cooperative and collective effort, performance measures will rise in several different ways.

The ambiance of any organization is intrinsically woven with relationships and cordial respect between the leaders and the other employees. It is the skill of most leaders to create good collaborative relationships that determine their position as firm leaders. However, by using the following skills, one can easily become a successful collaborative leader:

- Collaborative intention: Any business ordeal can not just be guided by emotional approaches. The debates that lead to the foundation should always be rational, and most importantly, the leader should always maintain a presence that is non-defensive. The leader has to make a conscious commitment to work with mutual respect for others. This non-defensive presence of the leader is often referred to as the Green Zone, which comprises people who seek building success using mutually agreeable solutions. On the contrary, Red Zone people are said to seek a defensive mode that is based on blame gaming. Problems should never be looked upon as battles, but should be dealt with in a manner that is collaborative, which can further enhance the relationships and performance in the long run.

- Self-Accountability: A collaborative leader should be responsible enough to take on the onus of one's actions and plans. Any business step can have unforeseen consequences which may be both intentional as well as unintentional. Negative thinking will only make the opportunities and choices in front of us invisible. True leaders must always be aware of the consequences that may be caused due to a choice that they make. Hence, they should always bring in the opinions of every group together and then make a final decision based on their intensive study and logic. Self-accountability will not only empower them with strong business ethics but will also make them more genuine in the eyes of the people who follow.

- Awareness: A genuine commitment to being self-aware and also, in the long run, to bringing reform to the work culture of an organization is needed in the mindset of a leader. Making effective choices to increase awareness among the other members of the organization is an essential skill that every leader has to be wary of. Situations may be different, and the objectives may vary accordingly. It is the leader who has to extend their hands to support the people in becoming self-reflective. Connecting with one's own inner feelings, values, intentions, and fears can have an incredible effect on the behavioral patterns of people. A leader has to dig into those emotions and find the main reasons that are the causes of the concerning behavior. A team can work at its best only when every individual is in a good mental and physical state. By increasing a sense of self-awareness among the people, a leader can make an effort to make them use those untapped emotions and skills for the benefit of the individual as well as the organization on a wider scale.

- Negotiating skill: One of the core business skills is the power of negotiation. Now and then, an organizational structure is bound to face a few bumps here and there. It is all up to the leader, who may avoid any form of conflict with the help of a complete denial attitude or can help bring a solution to the existing problems using perseverance and strategies. Every person can face difficulties in maintaining a relationship or a commitment, whether it is personal or professional. No matter how collaborative, accountable, non-defensive, truthful, and self-aware they may be, the lack of negotiating skills invites massive problems. Negotiating and working through a deal requires immense grit and confidence. The courage that is needed to pitch a deal and stick to the decision to further influence the minds of the people at the opposite end can be not only hard but can be highly risky as well. A collaborative leader has to have this skill of negotiation, without which the functioning of a business module can be an overbearing task.

- Trustfulness: Time and again, it has been proven that truthfulness helps in building any form of relationship. A leader has to have a truthful mindset, but they should also speak the truth at all times. Insecurities and distrust among the members of an organization are some of the major causes that lead to the dysfunction of a system. Listening is the key to understanding someone else's perspective, and if leaders are not patient listeners, they will be feared to be approached by the people. Such reasons can by themselves create numerous unnecessary communication problems and can raise difficult issues in the long run. An attitude of open-mindedness and an approach that is based on truth and honesty can help build a solid foundation between leaders and their followers.

Collaboration is all about working in mutual sync, and only with the ability to collaborate can you prosper in any field that you intend to join. The workforce is what makes the ground for the success of any organization, and if the people are taken care of in a professionally healthy way, then the outcome will be highly positive. By incorporating the idea of self-awareness, a collaborative leader can make people realize their self-worth and, in turn, create a trusting and fulfilling team environment.

7

Inspirational Appeal: Leading With Inspiration, Vision, and Value

Leaders who are inspiring have almost half of their work done toward their goal of accomplishing success. A large number of leaders are said to employ a wide range of tactics to reach their destination of triumph. Unlike rational persuasion, the inspirational appeal is designed to work by triggering feelings of enthusiasm and emotions.

Psychology plays a trick in evoking inspiration in the minds of people. The inspirational appeal works hand in hand with overwhelming feelings of longing to be like someone else or achieve what someone else has already achieved in life. The values and ethics set by a leader should be out in the open, accessible to the followers. This will generate a sense of connection that the people will feel towards the leader.

Since our childhood, we have all been asked about who our inspirations are and what we would like to be when we grow up. On a deeper level, these simple questions have greater depth attached. Since time immemorial, the minds of humans have been tapped with emotions concerning aspirations and dreams. People's feelings are adequate to develop a fervor for achievement in their minds when they are informed that if they persevere, they will very soon achieve their goals.

Characteristics of an Inspirational Leader

Inspiration is a great technique for influence. It is a method that makes a person control the minds of others without making any ruckus about it. It works on the foundation of an image that has been created over a prolonged period. This is because it is difficult for a person to instantly get inspired and accept another as a role model. It takes a certain time and mindset to observe the traits and achievements of other people and to be eventually captivated by the aura around them. There are no hard and fast rules that make a person inspirational. It is more about his or her inner skills and personality that do the trick. Nonetheless, what are the characteristics that lead to building a leader who believes in inspiration, vision, and values? Here are a few references to understand the concept behind it:

Inspiring actions

An inspirational leader is not only about giving motivational speeches. Preaching has to be done by putting set theories into action first. Every leader must demonstrate their willingness to be involved in minute details concerning the organization's and people's overall well-being. Any work environment is bound to get barraged with problems relating to service delivery or customer issues. It is when the tension remains high that the leader has to stay calm and work towards a solution with the utmost work ethics on display. Every reaction to any action is always followed by the observing people of any organization. During times of difficulty, a leader has to carefully set up meetings and present well-laid strategies to curb down the problems. It is this behavior of the leader that sets an inspirational example for the rest of the people. By observing this, the followers will also end up behaving with patience and calm during times of stress, just like their leader did.

Communication

Even the strongest of relationships can crumble down due to a lack of proper communication. Misunderstandings are the root cause of evil in any organization. The people who work for the organization should always feel secure. Even a hint of doubt or speculation can lead to a hysteria of confusion which may, in turn, cause a massive business disaster. Leaders have to make sure to include people in the decision-making process to a certain extent. By doing so, the leaders will boost their trust and give them a sense of security. The sensitivity of a person's integrity has to be dealt with the utmost care, and any decision that is made for change or anything else should be made in a systematic process without intending to harm the faith of the people. It is the ability of leaders to communicate their vision interestingly and clearly to the rest of the people that gives them a supportive audience.

Passion

Passion is what motivates people to endure and strive toward their objectives on a regular basis. There is a concept called shared passion. This emotion can be used by the leader to help generate passion in the rest of the people to aim and work towards a collective goal. A leader must inspire others to work passionately to become successful in life. The mission of the organization should also sync with the individual zeal of people to work hard for the goal. Very tactfully, a leader must make the rest of the people realize the purpose of working for something with great passion. By showing them a bigger scenario, a leader can persuade the followers to ignite their passion to bring in a magnanimous rate of success.

Listening

A leader cannot live in a bubble with no feedback or reviews. For people to grow vertically, they have to be open to listening to others' opinions about their leadership or anything related to the organization. An inspirational leader should always listen to the meaningful thoughts of the people, and by communicating in such a manner, the leader will be able to resolve many issues of the people in general.

The vision and mission of the leader and the organization must be in sync with the collective objectives of the people. It has been seen how leaders who are approachable in appealing are more likely to succeed in persuading others. Listening skills are an added quality that an inspirational leader should have. How can leaders believe they can inspire others if they are not aware of what the other end of the spectrum is thinking at the moment? To get the correct attention, they have to focus on breaking the ice caused by the hierarchical structure and introduce easier ways of adhering to the needs of the people.

Inclusion

When the employees develop a feeling of being left out, real problems start appearing within the organization. A leader has to make people feel inspired by including them in many matters. It has to be understood that inclusion does not only mean formal surveys and matters of feedback processes.

A leader has to understand the fact that it is the followers that make the position of the leader much more relevant. Therefore, based on a closer perception, much effort should be made on the leader's part to make the people feel needed and intimate with the organization. For example, involving the opinions of the people involved in making a simple decision about a process can help bridge the rift caused by the hierarchical structures. The general feeling is all about being considered a part of the organization, and getting included in many of the decisions affecting processes can help boost the morale of the rest of the employees to a great level.

Integrity and Trust

Integrity is what makes a person stand firm even at times of adversity, and trust is something that can change the dynamics of a relationship. As a leader, if you are not trusted by the larger sections of your followers, then that could cause considerable damage to your career and personal growth as well. The importance of trust and integrity cannot be lessened in any circumstance. People put faith in their leaders as they develop a sense of assurance from them. A leader has to be inspiring enough to create an ambiance based on respect and trust. It is a fact that trust cannot be built within a short period of time. It has to be worked on and proved over a period of time. The direction that a leader shows and the path that the followers take are not always the same, but it is the personality of the leader that can help them choose correct pathways. Every leader has to make an effort to live a life of integrity because their behavior and any decision that they make will always be carefully read by others. By doing so, they will be able to influence the minds of the people and make them more inclined to follow them into a positive space.

Considering what people want

The thought of rewarding outcomes can be a great driving force for people to work towards their goals. By understanding this psychological fact, leaders must do all within their reach to make their followers feel appreciated for their good work. Granting a raise in pay may not always be feasible, as that would require immense strategic planning and auditing. Therefore, leaders can, in their own way, organize rewards to recognize people with different capabilities and skills. Often, feedback disheartens people, and at such times, a simple pat on the back can work wonders to help boost their energy and confidence. Praise and recognition can make a person want more and will, in turn, make them give their best shot at work.

It is for all these reasons that people follow certain leaders and ignore others. Leadership is not always about a job title but is more of an inspirational position that has the power to influence the minds of many in a fruitful way. A truly inspirational leader is considered passionate, purposeful, a great listener, and someone who adds immense value to the role that they belong to.

The Art of Inspiring People

It is quite unlikely that a leader of a corporate giant would have thought about the complexities involved with the aspect of inspiring people. A CEO may be well versed in the tricks of the trade of the business they are involved in, but presenting oneself as a leader who focuses on encouraging and uplifting the thoughts of the followers may require more than what is anticipated. Inspiring people and donning the hat of an inspirational leader can never be a smooth sailing task.

Strong interpersonal skills, along with the ability to collaborate with the rest of the employees, are what give a boost to the power of a leader. The reason it is called art is that it requires an innate talent to get that aura of inspiration around your personality. Top-rated business people may be exceptional at striking million-dollar deals, but their ability to inspire other members of their organization might be very minimal. No doubt, to become a successful leader, business skills are very vital, but again, communication and the skill of having positive interactions can benefit in ways of their own. The point is some people may be technically sound, but when it comes to developing interpersonal relationships, they may be weak in maintaining a good rapport with others in general. This can be detrimental to the leader's popularity and even cause a blockage of opportunities in the near future.

Though it requires a lot of effort on the part of the leader, and to achieve the goal of becoming a leader who people look up to is not easy. However, here are a few points that could act as a reminder and guide them on their journey to excel in the art of inspiration:

- Positivity is the key to success.

- Open-mindedness goes a long way.

- With power comes responsibility.

- Gratitude is important.

- Being self-aware helps prevent ego issues.

- Respect everyone's integrity

Therefore, it can be said that it requires perseverance and several compromises to mold one into becoming a leader who is inspiring for the rest of the organization.

The Inspirational Leader

As we have mentioned already, what leadership is all about and how inspiration plays a part is so important in its implementation. A leader who chooses to lead with a vision and mission in mind has the potential to be the person who others choose to follow. Someone who understands the importance of having solid support from the followers and someone who is willing to take the necessary steps to keep their likes and dislikes aside to make ends meet for their followers is what inspirational leadership is all about.

The main agenda of an inspirational leader must be the continuous growth of the organization and its people. The leader should not only inspire the people with words but should try to bring significant changes to the workspace that could help sort out the work-life balance of the people. Being a firm believer in the core of values and business ethics, a leader must act as a role model for many to guide them to follow the right path.

Inspirational leaders are not just some other leaders. They not only delegate their decisions to their subordinates and their peers but are known for getting equally involved in every aspect of the process of management and people's engagement activities. The decisions that are made under their leadership are often seen to be coated with compassionate grounds, making it extremely feasible for the people with no power at all to thrive in the organization through just hard work. With an approachable vibe and no sign of fear-based tactics to manipulate the people, they are one of the most respected leaders. Inspirational leaders are believers in the inclusion of diversity, they treat mistakes as learning points, and they strongly believe in appreciating good work and effort.

8

How to Build a Legacy Leadership

We strive all our lives to build a life that we have always dreamt of. It is a never-ending process by which most ambitious people try to strike a balance between their personal and professional lives. The fast-paced lifestyle and the zeal to grow more and more towards achieving success often spare little time for anyone to think about what legacy they will leave behind after they are long gone.

It is a thought-provoking matter and can have a deep impact on the perspective of a persona based on their work and achievements. Legacy refers to something valuable that may be in physical or inspirational form, through which we may be remembered. The contributions that you make towards the different fields in your life add up to the person that you become in that process. A person's legacy may be associated with his or her way of thinking and the actions towards anything that is concrete. The concept of creating a powerful legacy can be an encouraging factor in determining the effort of the leader to continue working towards higher stakes.

Principles of Leadership Legacy

A powerful position, like a leader, is surrounded by heaps of tough responsibilities that tend to make leadership a demanding task. Most leaders reflect on the legacy they have created and left behind from time to time. So what can be counted as a legacy of a leader? This is something that can attract numerous kinds of critical thinking. Nevertheless, it can be summed up by saying that the decisions every leader takes during their lifetime may directly or indirectly have a marked influence on the legacy that they will leave behind.

A remarkable example of this aspect is that of the former CEO of GE, Jack Welch. According to Forbes, he once asked his employees to keep one question in mind while making decisions, and that was to ask whether what they were doing would bring a big win for the company? It is said that this question made a huge impact, and the earnings of GE went from $13 billion in the year 1981 to $480 billion in the year 2000. This is a clear example of how a leader can transform any business and workspace using the correct technique of influence.

Though there are no shortcuts to becoming an inspirational leader, some of the following legacy principles can help you understand the concept better and guide you in your efforts:

Engage employees

A prime reason why many organizations allocate some time to focusing only on employee engagement programs is that it is essential for the people who work day and night for a company to have a sense of belonging. Organizational boundaries are often set by the higher authorities in the hierarchical structure. It is the vision of the leaders that guides the way an organization functions.

Lack of communication and coordination between the different members of the organization can raise issues that may not be beneficial to anyone. Hence, a leader should always take the necessary steps to explain to the people what and why certain measures are taken. By having a clear idea about what the vision is, the leader can inspire people to work better for the new goals rather than create more confusion.

Focus

People are what make an organization work. Leaders have to be respectful of the human capital and should find ways to show their interest in their opinions and way of working. The main objective for a leader who is on a mission is to reach a wider section of the people involved in the functioning of the organization. Make sure to enquire about the unreachable sections of the workforce and then pay a visit to them personally. By making unannounced visits, you can see the real scenario of a workplace. When you as a leader take the initiative to get in touch with such people, make an effort to do it in such a way that no middlemen are involved in covering up the scene. In this way, you can check the ground reality of the condition of the workers, and by doing so, you can help them in manifold ways. Focus is the key, and by concentrating on the resources of your company, you will be able to set a good example for yourself as a leader.

Set the conditions

Laying down a condition of the environment that suits a hard-working employee can be another step in working towards the betterment of the organizational output. Legacy leaders should set working grounds for everyone working in the organization to excel in their area of performance. Here are a few ways in which you can set conditions as per the requirements of the team:

- Set goals as per the role and designations.
- Have a clear written code of expectations.
- Ensure that the job suits the skills of the employees.
- Enlist senior-level support.
- Understand the Human Resources policies.

Therefore, creating a set of terms for the smooth function of the processes can be very beneficial. There are many cases where people get the tendency to avoid verbally communicated orders, and at the end of the day, many tend to even forget. By setting up strong conditions like this, you will not only set your boundaries for yourself, but you will also be aware of the exact expectations of your current job role. By setting up conditions with clarity, many complications can be solved to a large extent.

Inspire

Some leaders are followed because of their inspirational personalities and the vibes that they project onto others. Leadership roles often function as change agents in the process of bringing new reforms. Change is a complex subject altogether and has the potential to create a pandemonium state of affairs. Legacy leaders will be remembered for the impact that they made on bringing about a new change while taking care of the people who followed them. It is how leaders use wit and intellect in handling a situation that makes them stand out from the rest.

Inspiration is a concept that works with no force or hardcore commitment, and is simply based on the respect that a person feels towards another. Such is the kind of respect that is earned and not at all manipulated by demand and can be considered as one of the most encouraging feelings to know that someone else feels inspired and motivated by you. The feeling that someone else wants to achieve goals like the way you did will act as an acknowledgment that something right has been done by you. This sheer feeling of motivation from an external source is bound to get you motivated and focused on setting a higher bar in return. The sole purpose of inspiration is to subtly create influence on another individual than any other source available.

Show where you stand

Self-advertisement is not a negative approach used in showcasing your performance as a leader capable of leaving a legacy of exceptional work behind. As crucial as it is to strive toward the organization's overall goal, it is also very important to highlight the work that you do to add more value to the organization. Similarly, with regards to the feedback that a leader should give on the performance of his or her subordinates, the leader should ensure to give them accurately and on time. The idea is to resolve and answer the various doubts that have been on the minds of people in the best possible way.

With timely feedback, an opportunity is given to the people to work on it and make amends as soon as possible. When feedback accumulates and is provided at a later stage, interest in working on it fades over time. Therefore, not many can focus and work on the feedback with equal determination as they would have done at the appropriate time. For example, a company called ResponseTek, a Vancouver-based company, introduced software that would help gather feedback of an employee from a consumer immediately. Each time a consumer bought their product, this company would send a message to the consumer's phone to ask how the particular salesperson performed. Finally, when the customer provided feedback, the employee was promptly contacted, providing them with information on which areas they needed to improve.

Legacy leaders should be aspirational and strive towards things that will leave their footprint. Most such leaders are seen actively taking part in knowledge transfer processes by sharing their expertise with the people who work for them. Therefore, it can be seen how different ways can help a leader become a legacy leader.

Building Leadership Legacy

A common fallacy is that legacy must be established near the end of a person's career, which is not the case. You can work towards creating a living legacy with the same might and passion. Even just the thought that makes you wonder about how impactful your life will be is exciting enough.

The various struggles and turbulences you face throughout your career will contribute to your ultimate success and failure. However, it is your overall caliber that will help you navigate through times of trials. Building a legacy is not only a step that you can take towards leaving a reputation after you leave but is also capable of giving a great sense of purpose to your life. The sweat that you put in to make your future years better can always be worth the effort.

The first step that you can take to build a legacy of leadership is by clearly writing down the goals that you would want to achieve in your lifetime. Focus on the goals that are of utmost priority to you and then think clearly about them for a while.

Defining leadership purpose

The idea of leadership can be very subjective. A person may be a leader in many ways. Defining the purpose of leadership is how you decide what leadership means for you and how you intend to build your leadership that matters the most.

We have examples of leaders who have left behind their legacy in different fields. Leaders with backgrounds in politics, technology, science, education, medicine, money, corporations, and the like have left their mark on history. However, defining and creating a legacy for yourself is not as easy as it sounds. The leaders who are considered to be legacy leaders have in their past achieved unattainable goals and have successfully brought reforms that have changed the lives of many. The point is that just by citing examples of renowned inspirational leaders, you cannot think of doing the same. Nearly every CEO and top management person would have earned the label of legacy leader if it was just for delivering inspirational speeches.

The opportunities that you get and the experiences that you earn in your lifetime are the building blocks for your career as a legacy leader. At the end of the day, no external factors can boost your career as much as your hard work and persistent effort to excel at your job. Nowadays, it can be seen that more and more people in leadership positions are keen on leaving a legacy tag for themselves. More so, what some of these leaders miss out on is that legacy is not something that you can achieve only after you leave the scene but is an ongoing process throughout your career.

The sense of purpose that is levied on leaders in the name of legacy is something to think about. Somehow, it is quite convincing to understand that many leaders become motivated to plan their roadmap for achieving higher goals in life to become legacy leaders in the future. As a result, there is absolutely no harm in making a relentless effort to achieve legacy leader status.

Questions to ask

Any attempt to learn something or achieve a goal requires a vigilant mind that asks countless questions. As they say, no question can ever be dumb. The fact is, how can you even think of going forward with your plans to become a legacy leader without even having a speck of doubt? To have questions in mind is completely normal and is also considered to be one of the best practices in order to learn more. When you begin pondering about how and why you would want the status of a legacy leader for yourself, you are sure to get hit with many types of queries. How can you think of becoming a legacy leader without having any worries? Questions are legitimate and should be asked; doubts should be resolved whenever they arise. Asking questions is the best that one can do to learn more.

Some of the few questions that may pop into your head are as follows:

- Why do I want to become a legacy leader, and what is it that makes me want to leave a footprint of myself even after I am gone.?

- As a legacy leader, how do I feel about leaving my work and business strategies behind?

- How would I want my business to turn up after a period of 3 or 5 years from now?

- What values, in particular, do I want to leave behind for my employees?

This question session does not have to be levied only on yourself. If you want, you can involve other trusted members of the organization to share their honest opinions with you. You could ask them the same questions and compare the various thought processes that will be reflected in all of their queries and answers. By making serious plans like these, you can push yourself towards becoming a legacy leader in all respects.

How I want to influence the world

A big concept may not always translate into a big leader. The manner in which those plans are carried out helps in developing the personality of the leader. Coming to the main point, how I, as an individual, would influence the world is a very subjective question. Some would say they would want a peaceful nation, whereas some would dream of earning more money. Not a single answer is bound to match because no two people's minds think the same way. To even try to compare the perspectives of two people regarding their personal goals will be an unwise effort. Hence, to pinpoint a particular desire on behalf of the many aspiring leaders can be unfair. However, an overall perspective of what measures could be taken to influence the world in a positive manner can be discussed in detail:

Try giving back to the society

Leadership is not only about securing the top position in a business setup or an organization of a different kind. Quality is something that not everyone can possess, or rather, it would take a long time for one to understand the intricacies involved in the making of a real leader. There are many such leaders who would aim not just to leave a legacy behind them, but would want to contribute to society as well. By investing in learning, most leaders throughout their lives spend a lot of time learning and many times unlearning the things that they thought were right. However, with time, they gain immense experience and knowledge, which they would want to give to new joiners and people aspiring to be leaders like them. Therefore, bypassing their hard-earned knowledge and anecdotes to make their experiences interesting, they intend to help the next generation achieve success.

Stand for causes

With the power possessed by leaders, it is possible to stand for causes that may benefit society in many ways. As a leader, within the organizational framework, you may raise your concern about the equality of pay among all the genders, and outside the workspace, you could stand up for any cause. It may not necessarily be a cause that would attract huge attention, but it can be a simple cause that may have the potential to benefit a certain section of the society that we live in. Therefore, by using power and influence in the right direction for valuable causes, a leader is definitely bound to be considered a legacy leader in the near future.

Unite employees

What is the point of having influence if you can't use it on your followers? Employees, no matter their job role, are all considered to be of the utmost importance to the organization for which they work. Most leaders are booming with new ideas and strategies, and they need employees to proceed with the implementation of those ideas. A leader must always be aware of the power of uniting with the employees. A group of people can be employed to spread the message of your vision with clarity, much like advertisements of sorts. By communicating with the members of your organization, you can influence the thought process of the employees you are in contact with regularly. You can be an inspiration for many only if you build that kind of reach for yourself, which requires a dedicated practice of communication.

Welcome diversity

An office with a global outlook is an ideal place to work. As a leader, you must ensure to set the balance between the different gender ratios' representation at work. People from different races, communities, sects, and religions should all be given an equal opportunity to thrive under your leadership. By hiring people from across countries and communities, as a leader, you will have access to different ideas and perspectives. Diversity can add a lot of value to the normal work process of the organization. An organization that has diverse employees has a higher chance of surviving and winning in different situations. Where different perspectives are at play, there is bound to be an interesting crowd. The ambiance of a workplace is made by its employees and when there is a varied mixture of skills and ideas, the organization is sure to flourish for the better.

Be interesting

There are too many people in the world who can preach the same vision that you have in mind. However, it is the manner in which you present your story to your audience that will make you interesting and accepted by many. A leader does not have to have a serious face all the time. As they say, respect has to be earned and not demanded. Therefore, it is quite logical that people will respect you as a leader if they like you as a person. When interacting with people, try to share a few personal and professional anecdotes here and there to ignite the interest of the audience. The more relatable they find their leader, the more they will tend to believe in him. And what better way to become a legacy leader than to be loved and remembered by countless people?

Practice kindness

What could be more attractive than a kind person in a harsh, competitive world? Kindness and empathy go a long way in making people feel secure and respected. By taking care of the feelings and well-being of the employees, a leader can also garner extreme support from the followers. By communicating with the employees without any attitude of arrogance and/or dominance, a leader can influence them in a positive way. Work can be done without creating a hostile atmosphere. It's a two-way psychological impact in which the receiver of a kind gesture returns the kindness. This method is one a leader can use to influence the employees to work as per his or her requirements without them feeling a tinge of stress.

Support others

Technology advancements and a growth in professional standards have made it easier to obtain technical assistance for any challenges encountered in any industry. However, to get human support, especially at work where competition is extremely high, is quite rare. People become so engrossed in their regular work lives that the connection between two people often tends to change with time and distance. This is a basic human issue that is faced by several others who have been working day and night for a living. A legacy leader can focus on an issue like this to bring about a change in a work culture in which people have become pretty accustomed. The balance between work hours and the time that one would spend with family, friends, and with oneself should be corrected. Such situations can be worked through with the collaborative effort of all the employees.

Advocate the importance of mental health

Globally, there has been a rise in the approach towards the conditions of mental health. Moreso, mental health awareness at the workplace is an absolute necessity. A true leader should always prioritize the health of every employee, including those suffering from various forms of mental health issues. Many times, stress and negativity at the workplace can also add to the anxiety that a person may feel and can pile on if kept unnoticed and untreated. A leader who aspires to be a legacy leader must consider prioritizing causes like this. Efforts should be made to make the work environment less frustrating and more positive. An open environment with engagement activities can be organized at times to keep people's minds off work and other personal stress and problems. Counseling and therapy sessions should also be provided as per the choice of the employees and strong emphasis must be made on the holistic wellness of the employees.

Monitor your impact

As a leader, careful monitoring of one's efforts, achievements, and progress towards the main goal should be done regularly. Keep a journal where you write in the data concerning anything related to your vision of the future. If need be, you can also interact with your peers and subordinates and get a review about how your work is creating an impact on them and the organization. Communicate with your seniors and stakeholders and get a clear picture of how they feel about your strategies and how they feel you should portray yourself. Constructive feedback should always be welcomed by a professional. Only by listening to what others have to say about you can you try to improve those areas that are causing you problems. Monitor each step that you take and check how it has an impact on your overall performance and image.

Seize small opportunities

No opportunity should be dismissed on the grounds of it being a small one. The underestimation of any chance can create a lot of regrets in the future. Every effort and every opportunity that comes along the way contributes to a positive outcome. Seizing even the tiniest of opportunities can bring unexpected results in the long run. A leader should not be prejudiced and should never judge a situation as a result of any bias. How you utilize even the smallest of opportunities for the cause of your team's goals shows your true spirit as a leader. No opportunity can, by itself, be small or big. It is how you perceive it that gives it the power to stand that tall. By accepting even the smallest of opportunities, doors towards bigger success can be opened.

Be an example

Change cannot come until and unless you take an active part in it. Similarly, no amount of good words can vouch for the reputation of a legacy leader other than the way he or she normally conducts. If leaders intend to become legacy leaders, they have to come to terms with the fact that no amount of accomplishments and wise words are more useful than the image of the leader, which is earned through many years of hard work and perseverance. People often look up to inspiring leaders and desire to be like them. This is why we have particular role models in mind. Many people are motivated to achieve their goals because they aspire to be like them. It is not easy to set an example. Every action you make will be scrutinized, but if you have the right motivation and goal in mind, you may actually set the bar so high that you will become an outstanding role model for future generations.

Keep your Legacy in Check

A consistent and relentless effort is needed for a leader to achieve the level of a legacy leader. With the daily work stress and overload of work, it is but natural to lose track of your goals every once in a while.

The work culture these days is such that it gives no time for an individual to focus on their goals other than the regular work projects. The delivery dates and the burst of emails throughout the day and week keep a person unpleasantly busy. So much so that finding time for one's personal needs, let alone pursuing any hobby or an activity, can become extremely difficult. However, as a leader who has the intention of leaving a legacy, you have to make time for yourself and cultivate a daily habit of self-reflection. Not necessarily do you have to give an hour or two for this. Just a mere 10 to 30 minutes can accomplish your purpose and can be highly beneficial. The main objective, though, is to keep yourself awake and enthusiastic about the dreams that you have for yourself. By reminding yourself again and again about your goals, your focus will not diminish and will keep you motivated enough to carry out all the needed exercises to work towards your goal.

Today, the lightning-fast internet, along with social media platforms, have created a vigilance of its own. Prominent leaders are often seen to be put under additional scrutiny by the press and people. Any summary offense on your part that may focus its shift on the company's reputation, along with yours, can affect the whole cause of building a legacy of leadership. Therefore, it is imperative to be cautious at all times and to live a life that is based on good morals and good work ethics.

Many CEOs, senior managers, and managers have also been spotted receiving counseling from executive coaches to help them achieve their aim of legacy leadership. The inclusion of coaches in this situation clearly signifies that their business is booming as their clients are gaining in number. Such an effort by the leaders demonstrates how the emotion of leaving a trace of yourself in the form of your work ethic and aspirations has had a global impact.

Individuals who wish to leave a legacy of leadership should keep in mind that they must work with an exceptional goal in mind. The stakes are very high due to the fierce competition, and many people are working with executive coaches to improve their leadership skills. It's very likely that everyone is striving toward the same goals. In such a situation, it is the tact of the individuals that will help them come out of this complexity. Legacy is just not created with mere thoughts and planning, extra work, and an out-of-the-box thinking approach must be used to get the strategy going. Leaders should stand out from the rest of their peers to be considered inspirational and legacy leaders.

Therefore, each leader should be self-aware and focus on the finest qualities that make them good people, both personally and professionally, in order to be a role model for the rest of the people. This introspection can guide them in charting a trajectory toward expanding their empire and becoming the finest legacy leaders.

Over to You

From the evolution of the world to the present day, leadership roles have carved out a niche for themselves. Leadership is a role that many have played throughout different walks of life, but only a few have managed to imprint their impression on the minds of the people. Leadership is a role that can be applied in many tiers. A person's capacity to form deep bonds with a big group of individuals is determined by one's magnanimous quality. Every race, color, creed, country, and profession has produced leaders who have influenced the lives of many people.

The power of influence, as we have seen in this book, is a topic that is too vast to be defined by one specific term. Similar is the word leader. Apart from the designated leaders in the different organizations, a leader can be a young girl fighting for environmental issues around the globe or an eight-year-old boy monitoring his class at school. A really inspirational leader is defined not by the position but by the mindset and the goals set for oneself. The value that leaders add to a simple situation and the guidance that they give to their fellow followers to increase their performance and improve their work-life balance is what sets the foundation of true leadership. The conduct and the traits of a leader decide whether he or she is liked by many or not. The aggregate view of the people regarding the behavior of the leader makes the leader likable. Interestingly, we learned that the more the leaders are liked by others, the more power they get to influence a wider audience.

The general theory is that a leader should be a peak performer and should not be limited to only a few mundane roles. Effective leaders should be proactive and should interact with every level of the workforce without any bias or vile attitude. They should be the ones who have played a huge part in the evolution of a team or a company. In recent times, the surge of influencers on social media platforms has dramatically changed the pattern of influence. Influencers are so named for a reason, as they have the widest reach that one could even imagine would be possible a couple of years ago. People are more drawn to the content created by the influencers. These days, people would rather go to social networking sites and watch promotional videos of products made by the influencers than watch advertisements on the television. Due to this booming industry of influencers, high-end brands of various products are also engaging several influencers to promote their products.

No doubt, the significance of influence cannot be overlooked in terms of creating an image and sometimes even doing the opposite. The interchangeable roles of power and influence are a tad bit tricky and can get their way out on numerous occasions. Power is nothing but the ability of an individual to have control over the mind and behavioral pattern of another. However, the resistance that comes with the introduction of a new change module is something to be understood concerning every given situation. No two situations are always the same, and dealing with the exact tact each time may not be a wise method.

In several cases, many confuse manipulation with the logic of influence. This doubt is shrouded by a thin line of difference because many relate influence with negativity. However, the relationship between influence and negativity is not entirely true because influence can be used to bring positive growth and changes in an existing organization. Such speculations can be put to rest with a leader who is inspirational and believes in bringing about significant change.

From the definition of power and influence to the different types of leadership roles, from the varied persuasion techniques to the defining purposes of leadership, from the inspirational aspect of influence to the rational model of analysis, from the building of a leader's true character to keeping the legacy leadership in check, we have all successfully dealt with every aspect that is concerned with the topic of power and influence which are relevant from the perspective of leaders and aspiring leaders of today.

The power that is vested in the position of the leaders makes them capable enough to bring about a massive change wherever necessary. More so, they can even make efforts to bring a change to the work culture, which may give them some bumps on the road. Again, emphasizing the importance of leaders does not mean that the duties of other organization employees are any less vital. With collaboration and bringing in serious consultation programs, leaders can bring about changes as effectively as they can. As a matter of fact, the influence that leaders mostly use is to instill a sense of compliance in the work ethics of the other employees. People issues and employee engagement programs are dealt with caution by the leaders in place. Therefore, it is the role of the leaders who help in bringing the team together; and they do so, by influencing the followers and other employees to strategically work according to the work plan.

By taking a closer look at the significant roles of leadership and their impact on the personal and professional lives of the employees and followers, a conclusion can be made that the power of influence is a skill that is difficult to harness, but possible to achieve with sheer dedication and confidence. At this juncture, it feels entirely right to reckon with the saying, "Leaders are always one step ahead but never leave anyone behind. Leaders are both born and made... to lead the rest to success."

References

13.3 The Power to Influence | Organizational Behavior. Lumenlearning.Com. https://courses.lumenlearning. com/suny-orgbehavior/chapter/13-3-the-power-to-influence/

Agile Vietnam. (2013). *Common influence tactics.* https:// agilevietnam.com/2013/01/04/common-influence-tactics/

Bazerman, M. H. (2020). *A New Model for Ethical Leadership.* Harvard Business Review. https://hbr. org/2020/09/a-new-model-for-ethical-leadership

Berger, J. (2017). *Invisible Influence: The Hidden Forces that Shape Behavior.* Simon & Schuster.

Berger, J. (2020). *The Catalyst: How to Change Anyone's Mind.* Simon & Schuster.

Big Think. (2021). *How leaders influence people to believe | Michael Dowling | Big Think* [Video]. YouTube. https:// www.youtube.com/watch?v=_Kv2vz1MQNA

Bloom, E. (2019). *7 Key Influence Strategies.* Office Influence. https://officeinfluence.com/7-key-influence-strategies/

Botha, T. *How does Leadership Influence Change in an Organisation?* ChangeFolio. https://changefolio.com/ articles/how-does-leadership-influence-change-in-an-organisation

Carnegie, D. (2012). *How to Win Friends and Influence People in the Digital Age*. Simon & Schuster.

Carter, L. *The 8 Questions To Ask To Create Your Leadership Legacy*. Louis Carter. https://louiscarter.com/the-8-questions-leadership-legacy/

CCL. (2020). *Master the 3 Ways to Influence People*. https://www.ccl.org/articles/leading-effectively-articles/three-ways-to-influence-people/

Cialdini, R. B. (2021). *Influence : The Psychology of Persuasion*. Harper Business.

City National Bank. (2019). *What's Your Leadership Legacy?* https://newsroom.cnb.com/en/business/leadership/leadership-legacy.html

Covey, S. R. (2004). *The 7 Habits of Highly Effective People*. Free Press.

Daskal, L. *How to Leave A Great Leadership Legacy*. Lolly Daskal. https://www.lollydaskal.com/leadership/how-to-leave-a-great-leadership-legacy/

DiFranza, A. (2019). *Collaborative Leadership: What It Is & Why It's Important*. Northeastern University Graduate Programs. https://www.northeastern.edu/graduate/blog/collaborative-leadership/

Drucker, P. (1996). *Your Leadership Is Unique*. Christianity Today International/Leadership Journal. https://www.edomi.org/wp-content/uploads/2021/01/your-leadership-is-unique-drucker.pdf

Eikenberry, K. *Five Ways to Influence Change in Others.* The Sideroad. http://www.sideroad.com/Business_ Communication/change-others-opinions.html

FemTech Leaders. (2021). *7 Influential Leaders Who Changed the World.* https://www.femtechleaders.com/ 7-influential-leaders-who-changed-the-world/

Feser, C. *When Execution Isn't Enough.* Mckinsey.Com. https:// www.mckinsey.com/~/media/mckinsey/featured %20insights/leadership/when%20execution%20isnt %20enough/when-execution-isnt-enough-chapter-3. pdf

Gavin Wedell. (2012). *What is Transformational Leadership?* [Video]. YouTube. https://www.youtube.com/watch?v= 60O2OH7mHys

GetSmarter. (2017). *The Difference Between Power and Influence.* https://www.getsmarter.com/blog/career- advice/difference-power-influence/

Gillis, G. (2014). *10 Great Communicators of the Modern Era.* Gerald Gillis. http://www.geraldgillis. com/10-great-communicators-modern-era/

Goleman, D. *The Power of Influence.* Korn Ferry. https:// www.kornferry.com/insights/this-week-in-leadership/ influence-emotional-intelligence

Hall, A., & Barrett, L. (2007). *Influence: The Essence of Leadership.* University of Nebraska Lincoln. https:// extensionpublications.unl.edu/assets/pdf/g1695.pdf

Impact Factory. *Leadership by Persuasion | Four Steps to Success.* https://www.impactfactory.com/library/ leadership-persuasion-four-steps-success

Indeed Editorial Team. (2021). *19 Influencing Skills (Plus Tips for Influencing Others).* Indeed Career Guide. https:// www.indeed.com/career-advice/career-development/ influencing-skills

Iwakiri, A. (2020). *One More on Power and Influence.* LAFRA. https://www.lafra.org/one-more-on-power-and-influence/

Jackson, T. (2022). *Leadership Skills: Persuasion and Influence.* About Leaders. https://aboutleaders.com/ leadership-skills-persuasion-and-influence/

Joel Garfinkle. (2019). *4 Powerful Qualities All Influential Leaders Have* [Video]. YouTube. https://www.youtube. com/watch?v=RHQiu-ovmcE

Kiger, D. (2017). *CEOs and the Art of Inspirational Leadership.* Business 2 Community. https://www.business2 community.com/leadership/ceos-art-inspirational-leadership-01791183

Kuhel, B. (2017). *Power Vs. Influence: Knowing The Difference Could Make Or Break Your Company.* Forbes. https://www. forbes.com/sites/forbescoachescouncil/2017/11/02/ power-vs-influence-knowing-the-difference-could-make-or-break-your-company/?sh=47e03d15357c

Kurter, H. L. (2020). *7 Powerful Characteristics Of A Truly Inspirational Leader.* Forbes. https://www. forbes.com/sites/heidilynnekurter/2020/02/29/7-

powerful-characteristics-of-a-truly-inspirational-leader/?sh=2892253ea05d

Llopis, G. (2014). *5 Ways A Legacy-Driven Mindset Will Define Your Leadership.* Forbes. https://www.forbes.com/sites/glennllopis/2014/02/20/5-ways-a-legacy-driven-mindset-will-define-your-leadership/?sh=4750991016b1

Maksimava, M. (2017). *6 science-backed ways to use emotional persuasion in marketing (with examples).* Awario Blog. https://awario.com/blog/emotional-persuasion-in-marketing/

Mills, G. R. (2017). *Mastering The Five C's Of Influential Communication.* Forbes. https://www.forbes.com/sites/forbescoachescouncil/2017/05/05/mastering-the-five-cs-of-influential-communication/?sh=5cd429a021b6

Mind Tools. *What Is Leadership?* https://www.mindtools.com/pages/article/newLDR_41.htm

Morgan, B. (2019). *The 10 Habits Of Transformational Leaders.* Forbes. https://www.forbes.com/sites/blakemorgan/2019/02/25/the-10-habits-of-transformational-leaders/?sh=7b064853343b

Morley, K. *How to effectively influence collaboration.* Karen Morley & Associates. https://www.karenmorley.com.au/influence-collaboration/

Mullin, S. (2020). *Emotional Persuasion: The Advanced Guide.* CXL. https://cxl.com/blog/emotional-persuasion-guide/

Rampton, J. *7 Tips to Make a Positive Change in Your Life.* Inc. https://www.inc.com/john-rampton/7-tips-to-make-a-positive-change-in-your-life.html

Riboldi, J. *5 Ways You Can Influence Positive Change at Work and in Life.* Ivy Exec. https://www.ivyexec.com/career-advice/2016/5-ways-can-influence-positive-change-work-life/

Rovers, L. H. *Three Easy Steps To Positively Influence Others.* Workplace Matters. https://www.workplacematters.ca/three-easy-steps-to-positively-influence-others/

Sagor, R. D., & Rickey, D. L. (2012). *The Relentless Pursuit of Excellence: Lessons From a Transformational Leader.* Corwin.

Scott, T. (2015). *How to Use Emotional Triggers to Increase Conversions.* Conversion Sciences. https://conversionsciences.com/how-to-use-emotional-triggers-to-increase-conversions/

Stack, L. (2016). *Rational Persuasion: An Effective Tool for Turning Your Ideas into Our Ideas.* The Productivity Pro. https://theproductivitypro.com/blog/2016/04/rational-persuasion-an-effective-tool-for-turning-your-ideas-into-our-ideas/

Steever, S. (2021). *Micro-Influencers Have A Story To Tell — Can They Help You Tell Yours?* Forbes. https://www.forbes.com/sites/forbesagencycouncil/2021/06/11/micro-influencers-have-a-story-to-tell---can-they-help-you-tell-yours/?sh=52104ab57600

Sunstein, C. R. (2016). *The Ethics of Influence: Government in the Age of Behavioral Science.* Cambridge University Press.

Tamm, J. *Collaborative Influence*. Radical Collaboration. https://www.radicalcollaboration.com/articles/collaborative-influence/

TEDx Talks. (2019). *How Influencers Have Transformed Modern Marketing | Rachel David | TEDxVancouver* [Video]. YouTube. https://www.youtube.com/watch?v=gbbEXnRG9d8

The Balance Careers. (2019). *Inspire People to Great Performance? You're a Leader Worth Following*. https://www.thebalancecareers.com/leadership-inspiration-1918611

Upchurch, D. (2017). *3 Ways to Live Your Leadership Legacy*. Training Industry. https://trainingindustry.com/articles/leadership/3-ways-to-live-your-leadership-legacy/

Villanova University. (2021). *What is Ethical Leadership?* https://www.villanovau.com/resources/leadership/what-is-ethical-leadership

Wikipedia contributors. (2022). *Transformational leadership*. Wikipedia. https://en.wikipedia.org/wiki/Transformational_leadership

Wooll, M. (2021). *Power versus Influence: How to Build a Legacy of Leadership*. BetterUp. https://www.betterup.com/blog/power-vs-influence

Zenger, J., & Folkman, J. (2015). *7 Things Leaders Do to Help People Change*. Harvard Business Review. https://hbr.org/2015/07/7-things-leaders-do-to-help-people-change

Printed in Great Britain
by Amazon

19623453R10081